TAKE CHARGE OF ⬛⬛⬛⬛⬛⬛⬛⬛⬛⬛⬛,
BECOME IRRESISTIBLE AND MAKE A BIGGER IMPACT

PERCEPTION

FRANZISKA ISELI & CHRISTO HALL

Edited by Wendy & Words (www.wendyandwords.com)
Cover design by The Business Hood (www.thebusinesshood.com)
Text design, typesetting and e-book by BookCoverCafe (www.BookCoverCafe.com)
Published by TCK Publishing (www.TCKPublishing.com)

First edition 2016

© Copyright 2016 Franziska Iseli and Christo Hall

ISBN:
978-1-63161-981-6 (pbk)
978-1-63161-982-3 (ebk)

CONTENTS

INTRODUCTION

People either want you or they don't. What makes them want you – or not – is how you are perceived by them. Perception is in fact the key to making yourself – or your brand, products or services – irresistible!

Let's start off with a little story. (You'll find, as you work through this book, that we share a few stories. That's because stories are one of the greatest ways to remember and learn something.)

Back in the 1980s, there was a Dolly Parton lookalike contest held in California on Santa Monica Boulevard. Guess who slipped into the competitors' line-up? That's right, Dolly Parton herself.

Think about this for a moment. A lookalike contest is a judged event. It's all about perception. In order to win a lookalike contest, you have to influence the judges' perception of you. You don't have to **be** the best; you just have to make the judges **believe** that you're the best – in this case, the best and truest version of Dolly Parton.

So of course the real Dolly won, right?

Nope.

In this competition, two people (and drag queens at that, since it was a drag queen contest!) were able to convince the judges that they were better versions of Dolly Parton than Dolly herself. Sure, Dolly may have been the real thing. However, she wasn't able to convince the judges that she was the **best** thing. The perception was that there was someone else better; in fact, there were two "someone-elses" who were better at herself than herself!

Pretty amazing! But how does this apply in the real world? To your world?

Well, in fact, this same situation occurs everywhere – with people, with businesses, and with products. It doesn't matter *how* good you are; if the people you are aiming to positively influence – your target market – don't perceive you as such, it could all be for naught.

Let's take two competing consultants, for example. One might have very high qualifications and more experience than the other, and be quietly beavering away, doing great work. Like Dolly, she is the "real deal." But if her "less-qualified" competitor is busy putting himself out there, creating a positive image of himself and getting people to talk about him, he may well end up being perceived as better than the one who is the "real deal" – and out-competing her in the market as well. It seems unfair, doesn't it?

Likewise, a product may be heavily marketed. You hear of it often and begin to trust it: it's everywhere. Everyone seems to be using it, so it must be good, right? It becomes a bestseller, and meanwhile the world's best product (that no one has heard of) is sitting right beside it on the store shelf, with its manufacturer gradually going out of business.

We're not saying that the quality of your product or service doesn't matter; of course it does, hugely! However, quality alone is not enough to make you successful in your workplace or to make your product sell or people desire you. You also need to be able to manage how you are perceived. Being the real deal is great, but you also need people to perceive that, know it, and to believe it. This is *so* important. Otherwise, you are doing a disfavor to the world if you have a great product or service but no one knows about it. And it's a disservice to **you**!

Perception matters. Immensely.

Perception, although it exists only in people's minds, can even alter reality. That's because perception can totally change what people do or don't find irresistible. Allow us to tell you another little story to illustrate this.

This tale comes from Australia where there is a discount clothing store called Best & Less. Best & Less wanted to get away from the negative perception that shoppers have of their brand: that their products are of a poor quality. So, in a very clever marketing ploy, they pranked consumers by setting up a fake storefront at an upscale shopping mall in downtown Sydney.

They called the new store L&B and branded it with an expensive-looking logo. They designed the store to look like a pricey boutique, with floor-to-ceiling glass windows and a classic, minimalist décor inside. The giant black L&B logo was displayed on the front glass doors and also embossed on shimmering gold shopping bags.

However, the store was stocked with regular Best & Less clothing. No different except for a much smaller range of products being offered and the prices were nearly quadrupled.

Shoppers came in and sifted through the racks of clothing. To their surprise, though, when they brought their items to the cashier, the first digit on each price tag was ripped off. The cashier explained with a smile that a dress, for example, was actually $40, not $140. The shoppers' responses were recorded on video.

"Why is that?" one shopper asked nervously, as if assuming something must be wrong with it.

"Because this is actually a Best & Less store," the cashier explained.

The shoppers' reactions were priceless! (Pardon the pun.)

"I don't mean to be a snob, but I wouldn't go to Best & Less," said another shopper. And then she paused ... "But that's the point, isn't it?" She got it.

Another exclaimed, "Oh my god ... they're changing my perception!"

And she was exactly right: it was all about perception. People who would never have set foot in a Best & Less, because of their **perception** of what that store is, were pranked into coming inside. And they liked it! In a brilliant piece of marketing, the "L&B Experiment" video was played on national television ... and the perception of the Best & Less discount clothing store was changed across the nation. (You can watch the two-minute video yourself; just head over to this book's web page via the link at the end of this book.)

This is why the title and focus of this book is *Perception*. Knowing how to utilize the power of perception is **the key to getting noticed, liked, and wanted.** You are going to learn that:

- anything is possible through perception (well, almost anything)
- you have the choice and power to influence and even completely change others' perception of you, your products, and your business.

In fact, knowing how to change perception (how you perceive a certain situation or circumstances and how people perceive you) has **everything** to do with being more successful in all areas of life: your career, your business, your money, your relationships, and your lifestyle.

(And hey, by the way, we like to keep things simple. So from now on when we use the word "you," we are referring to whatever applies to you in either the personal or professional sense, including your business and your brand, products, ideas and/or services.)

Perception is your vehicle to achieving whatever you set out to achieve. And that is why we have written this book. Not only to help you understand the importance of perception, but **how** to ensure that you are creating the right perception of yourself, both in the market and in life, to get better results all around.

In business those better results are, of course, more sales and a more desirable brand! In this book you'll learn how to differentiate your product, or service, or **you** (if you're the product) and communicate that so your target market sees you and likes you! You'll also learn how to apply these principles internally, so that you attract the right kind of people and opportunities to you to create the life and business you desire. In short, you and your business will become i r r e s i s t i b l e.

Sounds pretty good, right?

Why listen to us?

Okay, you've stuck with us this far. But by now you're probably wondering, *Who are these guys? Why should I listen to them?*

In short, we are a pair of entrepreneurs, mad adventurers, and authors, as well as a husband-and-wife team. Allow us to introduce ourselves and what inspires us to do what we do.

Franziska is a Swiss-born Australian who works to make the secrets of "the big guys" marketing and branding available to the small business world. She is a bit of a rebel and an incredible visionary, with an amazing ability to see ahead and predict trends. And she uses that foresight to create plans and strategies executed with the precision of a Swiss clock. She's got a flair for putting all the pieces together, overlooking nothing to create impactful marketing campaigns. She is known for her authenticity, courage, and infectious energy.

Christo is the down-to-earth guy with a track record for turning those big ideas into reality. He's been entrepreneurial his whole life, proudly claiming never to have held a "real job." (Unless you count being a professional surfer for seven years as a real job.) He's got a knack for recognizing profitable business ideas and transforming them into reality. He has added millions of dollars to his clients' revenue streams by assisting them in implementing powerful new marketing strategies and systems.

We run a few different companies and one of them, Basic Bananas, is a leading global marketing education organization. We've worked with thousands of entrepreneurs, business owners, and individuals from around the world, and have been honored with business awards and invitations to present our ideas on stages globally including TEDx. We're regularly featured in global publications including the Huffington Post, Business Review Weekly, The Sydney Morning Herald, The Age, Channel 9, BRW, 2UE, and The Daily Telegraph.

We believe that one reason we resonate well with our crowd is our no-BS approach. We love pushing boundaries, and we refuse to simply follow the rules of convention just because "that's how things have always been done." Doing things differently is so much more fun (and fruitful!).

Speaking of fun...

Fun is something we both love. A lot. Work is far from the only thing in life (and for most of us, it's not even the most important thing). For us work has to be fun and integrate with things we love. We both make time for lots of fun, surfing almost every day, playing music with our band, Salty Lips, and spending several months of each year traveling around the world, meeting up with amazing people for crazy adventures. And we know that "business" and "fun" are not mutually exclusive, at all. We encourage everyone we work with to inject the "fun factor" into all aspects of life – including your business. Because fun is fun!

The birth of this book

Okay, so that should give you an idea of where we're coming from and what we believe in. But why are we doing this?

We've been enjoying our diverse experiences in the business world – building our various businesses and seeing them grow and develop. But what we've found is most important to the two of us personally are the relationships we have developed over the years, and the learning curve that goes along with each of those personal stories – both for our clients and us.

What has driven us to write this book is the growing list of success stories from our business owner clients who, after applying some of our frameworks, see a complete change – within themselves and their business. Of course, everyone's story or journey is different. However, we have noticed some common threads in all of them: in particular, **the importance of taking charge of how you are perceived** by employing the strategies we explain in this book, to help you to achieve greater success.

(Just to clarify, when we use the word "success" we mean whatever means success to **you**! For some it's to make more money; for some it's to spend time with loved ones; for some it's to live on an island in the middle of nowhere; and for some it's spending time in their veggie garden. While a big chunk of the book is about business success, the positive perception principles we share apply to any vision of success you hold.)

This book is our opportunity to give back by sharing our learning. We're humbled to work with such amazing people, both on our team and as clients. The two of us have learned an immense amount along our journey thus far, with a lot more to come. We have helped many of our clients from around the world achieve success and transform their lives ... It's these stories, and the impact we've been able to make, that make us wake up with a big smile.

Who will love this book?

When we started Basic Bananas, we went into business as a marketing company, aiming mainly to help entrepreneurs and small business owners. However, what we have discovered is that many of our strategies relating to perception, which we initially developed to help business owners, also help people in their daily lives: be it rising up the ladder and winning that promotion or becoming more successful in relationships – even love!

So that's what we mean when we say that this book is for **you**. No, we may not know you personally (make sure you come and say hi over on our social media sites or in person so we can meet you!), but that doesn't matter because the techniques we share are universal. From those striving to sell more of their product or grow their company to those seeking to improve their personal lives, perception is important to everyone.

This book is for the entrepreneur who wants to think outside of the box. It's for the business owner who wants to turn their company into a magnet for their dream clients. (Yup, there is such a thing.) And it's for **everyone** who wants to achieve their aspirations in life and love and to achieve their own version of happiness.

As we mentioned, we love stories! Human beings for centuries have communicated learnings through storytelling. We know it works. So that's how we are have structured this book – with each chapter beginning with a segment of a story. Our three main characters are all fictional but are based upon truth. Brook, Danielle, and Max – and their dilemmas and their solutions – are all inspired by **real** people, **real** situations, and the **real** relationships we have cultivated through Basic Bananas.

We'll alternate their story with our advice and recommendations, so you can discover from these examples exactly how you can apply the concepts of influencing perception to your own business, as well as to your personal and professional life. This will entail determining what perception you want to cultivate – your brand personality – who you are trying to reach and how you can influence, amplify, or even change that perception. And why! You are going to discover that you can pretty much achieve **anything** by understanding, and applying, the power of perception.

The world needs you and your brilliance! And **you** have the power to determine people's perception of you and your awesomeness. We've got a lot of ideas and information we want to share. So, let's get stuck into it.

Why Perception

"Joanna! Where are the accounting summaries?" Brook's fingers raced through the filing cabinet. She called out in the direction of the hallway. "Joanna!"

Joanna flew in.

Brook was desperate. "I need the annual summaries. Now! Where's Janice?"

"It's Tuesday, Brook. She's not in." Joanna looked over her shoulder then back to Brook, who was still frantically rifling through the filing cabinet drawers. "My phone's ringing. It's probably about the Falucci contract. Are you okay if I get it?"

Brook looked up. "Sure. But new contracts aren't going to help us if I can't pay you," she said, just a tad tersely.

Ming peeked her head around the corner. "Brook, what's going on?" she asked, as Joanna high-tailed it back to her desk and picked up the phone.

Brook slammed the cabinet drawer shut and opened one below it. "My bank meeting. It's in twenty minutes. If I don't get this loan, this whole company is screwed."

"Brook," Ming said, "just breathe. I'll go look in Janice's office."

Ming returned with an armful of file folders.

"But these aren't the summaries," said Brook.

"It's all the same information." Ming glanced at her watch. "And besides, you've got to go."

"Oh god," sighed Brook. "Okay, thanks." She shoved the files into her bag and strode out.

But Joanna intercepted her at the door, phone in hand and quickly pressing the mute button. "Mr. Falucci wants to talk to you."

"Tell him to talk to Sam." Brook grabbed her coat.

Joanna thrust the phone. "He said you, specifically."

"Sam!" Brook called. "Phone!"

She turned to Joanna. "Let him know that Sam's our senior designer, budding star, whatever. It can't always be me anymore."

"Brook!" urged Ming. She was standing at the open door. Her eyes were wide. "Go!"

Brook secured the bag under her arm and started to run.

"Good luck!" one of them shouted after her.

Danielle felt like she had taken a flying brick in the front of her head. No, she realized, it was actually the other way around. She wanted to be the one throwing that brick. At Rudy.

18

Danielle clenched her fingers around her coffee mug, willing it to remain there safely.

"Congratulations, Rudy." She even smiled.

"I know!" he said, with an uncharacteristically wide grin. "I thought it would be you, Danielle, honestly I did. You've been here so much longer than I have!"

The coffee seemed to be dancing in her cup, forming a little fountain in the center. Danielle forced herself to look up.

Rudy twirled out of her office. She could hear him singing as he pranced down the hall. "I'm moving to the corner suite!"

Un-be-lievable.

Danielle was smarter than Rudy. She worked harder than him, getting there earlier than him every day. She definitely dressed better than Rudy, in his stupid grey and brown suits every day. Who even designed that crap? And she had helped him with his accounts more than once! Not that Mr. Robertson knew that.

Nine years as "just" an accountant.

Fifth time passed over for promotion.

She must be setting some kind of company record.

"Arggghhhh!"

Oh god. Did she really just do that?

Her mobile was ringing. She picked it up and saw it was Max. *Sorry bro, you can wait.*

Danielle put down her phone and looked up. Marie was peering in her door, her eyes wide. "You okay?"

"I'm good," Danielle replied. Too quickly. "Just got a paper cut," as she fumbled with some paper. "I'm good. Thanks."

Brook tried not to slump in the chair as she listened to the same lines she'd heard before. *Do bankers all read the same handbook on how to reject people?*

"Your company..."

"*Designs by Brook*," she offered.

"Ah yes." Mr. Vogel looked down and scribbled something in his note pad. "*Designs by Brook*."

Is he smirking? "But I'm expanding," she offered. "It'll be two separate companies. Expanding the original interior design one and opening the new import business."

Mr. Vogel twiddled his pen.

"That's why I need the loan," she continued.

"I'm sorry, Ms. umm..." Mr. Vogel (*hmmm more like Mr. Grump* thought Brook) searched his notes. He looked up. "Brook. I just don't see that you meet the criteria, Brook. I don't see that the numbers add up."

"But they *do* add up," she protested. She reached down to her handbag and plunked the stack of files on his desk. "My sales have doubled each of the last three years. Look, I can show you."

Mr. Vogel eyed the stack of papers. He leaned back.

"Please," she continued. "Please look. All the information is right here."

"Our minimum requirements are there for your protection. We don't want to put you in a position where you're unable to pay back your loan."

Brook opened the top folder. "I'll show you. Let me find last year's sales." She flipped through the pages. Mr. Vogel folded his hands and watched her.

"Actually, here, this page. The Indonesian imports. The material costs are so low, it's guaranteed to turn a profit." She held a sheet of paper out to him, but his hands remained on his lap. "Provided you give me the loan. So I can run it at the appropriate scale."

Mr. Vogel was looking at his watch.

"Please," Brook said, trying not to sound like she was begging. "The numbers work out. And I already have the clients who want the product. I just need ..."

Mr. Vogel stood up and held out his hand. "Thank you, Ms., umm, Brook. We'll get back to you."

Back in her car, Brook thrust her key into the ignition then slumped in the seat. She was at a loss. Her business was, by every definition, successful. Sam had worked out great. Only ten years younger than she was, but with such a different perspective on things – a different eye and a different approach. And now with Ming and Gustavo on the design team, too, she was up to five employees. Well, four and a half, with Janice still part-time.

And *Designs by Brook* was getting such great attention. She'd been named one of the nation's top new interior designers to watch. There'd been a small magazine story last year and the feature in *Urban Style* was supposed to be coming out next week.

So why were the banks so reluctant to acknowledge that? Growth requires investment, right? Taking Joanna on had paid off right away in saved time. Brook could focus on the clients and the actual designing. Taking on a second designer had seemed more of a risk at the time, but Sam had also worked out well.

But now with Ming and Gustavo, she was committed. Four and a half salaries to pay, not to mention her own. One bad month and she wouldn't be able to afford it all. And how would she ever get the Indonesian imports happening without financial investment? Not to mention that she was well overdue to move up from that little office.

Why was it so hard to get a loan officer to see things the way she did?

Brook picked up her phone. "Dani? I don't want to bug you at work. You free for a coffee after?"

Danielle snorted. "You free for something stronger? What a day!"

"Actually, Roger's away for a few days. We could do dinner if you want."

"I'm yours. Casa Pedro's at seven?"

When you meet someone new, do you know that they form their opinion of you within the first few seconds? This is a fact that's so important to understand as it holds true not only socially, as in who wants to be your friend, but also to those with the power to make major decisions about your future. People such as a prospective employer or the bank manager who will decide whether or not to grant Brook her "life-altering" loan. Not to mention your potential clients.

Numerous studies have shown that people judge one another almost instantly, based on how they sound and how they look, even from just viewing photographs. Those seemingly superficial attributes quickly influence us to come to conclusions regarding personal characteristics such as trustworthiness, intelligence, social status, and even promiscuity. We're talking about perception.

Whether those opinions are right or wrong is another story. But the point here is you cannot get around the fact that **others will always have some sort of perception of you or your business.**

First impressions are clearly important. However, you do have opportunities – numerous opportunities, in fact – to alter people's perception of you.

Defining perception

It's important to understand everything the word "perception" encompasses, so you can harness its power! First, a quick

English lesson with the Merriam-Webster dictionary*, which provides three versions of their "simple" (a.k.a. plain-English) definition – and all three are important. Here they are, along with a few of our thoughts:

- **Perception is the way you think about or understand someone or something.** In other words, perception does not necessarily equate to factual reality. Like that saying about beauty, perception exists only in the mind of the beholder. It is how someone *else* thinks about you or understands you.

- **Perception is the ability to understand or notice something easily.** So perception also ties in with being noticed. If you, your business, or your products are not on someone's radar ... well, they don't even have a perception of you at all! No one is thinking about you, much less talking about you.

- **Perception is the way you notice or understand something using one of your senses.** Perception exists in your mind, but the basis for that perception (the "data") comes from your sensory input. You see that newest iPhone and you fall in love with the design. You taste that new potato chip flavor and find it irresistible, or you hear one of your good friends talking about what a great guy John is and you suddenly want to hang out with him.

---

* www.merriam-webster.com

Your senses provide you with the information to enable you to form an opinion. They create your perception.

Perception creates reality

Perception can and does influence reality. Let's say you are a shy person, tend to fidget when you talk and have trouble making eye contact. Although these behaviors are only a result of your shyness, they might lead people to perceive you as untrustworthy. Yet their perception may not **be** the reality; it may be completely wrong!

Their perception that you are untrustworthy, however, will **influence** your reality. It will most likely cause you problems in life, in everything from forming friendships to succeeding at business deals.

> **Perception may or may not be the reality.**
> **But, good or bad, it can create a new reality.**

And that is how learning about perception, and the art of deliberately influencing perception, can help you live the reality you want. Understanding perception, and specifically the power you have to influence how others perceive you, is an essential tool in achieving **your** definition of success – no matter what success means to you: money, recognition, freedom, or just partying your pants off.

Taking control

Changing perception is all about getting you, or your business, from where you are now to where you want to be. Sure, perception exists only in the minds of other people (and your own!). But that doesn't mean that how you are perceived is out of your control. There are many things you can do to influence the perception others have of you!

Your "right people"

Your aim is to make your brand, and your products or services, irresistible to the right people: the people you want to attract.

If you are already in business, you have probably worked out some sort of business plan that identifies your target clientele. These are who we mean by "the right people." Now by this we're not saying that the other people are wrong! It's just a term to define the demographic that you are trying to reach: the people who want what you have to offer and who you want to attract. Luckily, you have the power to choose who you want to work with!

If you are selling expensive women's designer shoes, it is not much of an issue if most men have no perception of your business or products. They are not your "right people." It's not even a big deal if lower-income working women have little perception of your product because your target client is an affluent woman who can afford your shoes. On the other hand, if your product is a book of quick-to-cook, healthy recipes, you'd better make sure those working moms *do* hear about you – and that their perception of your product is positive.

Who are they?

It's a very interesting fact that different people have different perceptions of value versus cost – even between those with the same disposable income.

Let's look at an example: two friends, Rosie and Saba. They are both single working women, earning a decent income and without dependents. So they each have a fair amount left over at the end of each month and can afford some treats in life.

Rosie is into Saint Laurent handbags. She prides herself in being well dressed and being known among her friends for having good taste. She likes the message that her expensive handbags and other classic accessories send out. For her, paying $5,000 or more for a handbag is totally worth it. Her handbags make her feel good: she belongs to the "Saint Laurent Club"! To Rosie, the perceived value of the bag outweighs its cost many times over.

Saba, on the other hand, thinks that it's outrageous that Rosie would pay $5,000 for a purse. But Saba spends at least $5,000 a year flying to tropical resorts, to get a few days off being pampered in the sun. Rosie absolutely doesn't get it: Why would Saba pay all that money for flights and hotels and it's all over in a few days? In the end, Saba has nothing to show for it. At least Rosie has her handbag collection.

It's all about perception. What one person sees as valuable the next person may see as waste. Rosie values how awesome she feels as she walks the streets with her Saint Laurent handbag. Saba values the freedom and excitement she experiences when she hops on a plane and the chance to escape from her day-to-day life, coming home with long-lasting memories.

Before you put too much effort into trying to change perception, you first have to make sure that you know *whose* perception you have in mind: that you are targeting your "right people." If you make designer handbags, you don't want to waste your energy trying to convince Saba. You need to reach Rosie.

What do they want?

Different cultures have different ways of perceiving things. For example, some nationalities are known to be more punctual than others that are more laid-back. When you are defining your "right people," it's important to take into account any cultural differences between different countries, or between different ethnic groups within the same country, or even between city and rural residents. There are also different business or corporate cultures, religious cultures, regional cultures, and artistic cultures. Imagine being a fly on the wall at a meeting of banking CEOs compared to one of indie music producers with all the different standards in behavior, manner of dress, how they speak, even what they order for dinner. Danielle may look down on Rudy's "stupid" grey and brown suits, but they probably actually fit in quite well in the culture of their conservative accounting office.

When working at changing perception, you must pay attention to the habits and norms and values of your target clientele, and remember that these may not be the same as your own. Here's a great example: Two hugely successful international airlines, both of which fly roughly the same routes. You would think that they would be competing for the same clientele. However, instead, they use the power of branding to cultivate a perception that is attractive to different subsets of their market; they can be slightly overlapping, of course.

Qantas, the largest Australian airline, projects an image of being safe, professional, and conservative: perfect for their target clientele. They attract corporate travellers, business professionals, and families – people from cultures that value that perception of reliability, predictability, and safety.

Virgin Airlines fly almost the same routes as Qantas, especially throughout Australia. But they project a completely different image. They are quirky, hip and fun. In fact, as we wrote this, we went over to their website. Their booking page says "Cheers to a trip. Get out of town with awesome low fares." We don't think you'll ever see that type of copy on the Qantas website; it wouldn't be in line with their brand. So Virgin attracts a different demographic: a younger crowd, entrepreneurs ... a culture of travellers who are out to have fun.

It's all about knowing who your "right people" are and then projecting yourself in such a way that you are influencing their perception of you! Suddenly they can see you clearly, perceive your points of difference, and find you relatable and irresistible! You have what they want.

Through harnessing perception, you have the power to change reality!

Perception and Reality

"**S**omething to drink?" the waiter asked.

"I'll wait for my friend," Brook started to say, as Danielle strode in, elegant as always in a purple satin Armani dress.

"Sorry, I was late leaving work," she said, pecking Brook on the cheek as she sat down. Danielle looked up at the waiter. "Two margaritas. House size."

"How do you walk in those things?" asked Brook. "You look great! As always."

"Yeah, well maybe I should start wearing mousy little no-name business suits. That creepy little new-start got my promotion."

"What? That's not fair. I think those old bosses of yours are sexist."

"It would actually be easier if that was it. But it happened last year with Margo too. She got promoted ahead of both Rudy and me."

Danielle shook her head as she continued. "I don't know what it is. I had four years on Margo. And two on Rudy."

The margaritas arrived and the two friends clinked their glasses. "Here's to whatever," said Danielle. "So anyway, what's up with you? How's the exciting world of interior design?"

"Oh god, I am so done with this, Dani."

"But you're doing so well! You've grown so much this past year; you're a boss and everything. And you got all those awards."

"One award."

"That New Designer one and the Entrepreneur of the Year one. That's two at least."

"Whatever. Awards don't pay the bills. Sure I'm a boss now, but that just means I'm responsible for covering all these extra salaries. It's pressure." She shrugged. "I have great clients; they love me. Actually, too much. I'm trying to get Sam to take over more of the new projects, right from the initial meetings and brainstorming."

"See how wonderful you are?" Danielle looked down at her drink, swirling the ice around. She looked up. "Well, it does make sense that they want *you*. It is 'Designs by Brook'. "

Brook thought of stupid, smirking Mr. Vogel. "Yeah, I was thinking maybe I've outgrown that name. Anyway, I had another meeting about getting that loan. Different bank this time."

Danielle met her eyes. "And...?"

"I don't know, Dani. Partly I feel good. The numbers all add up; I can't see why they would say no. I need that loan."

"Oh, that's for your import idea, right?"

"Well, even to cover monthly costs, salaries and all that for Designs by Brook. But yes, the imports. Sam had a great idea, by the way. He thinks I should break the import business off as a separate company. He's even got a name for it: Savvy Mundo."

Danielle chuckled. "That sounds like the kind of name Sam would come up with."

"I kind of laughed at first too. But I actually like it. And, like he says, it gives more options, not tying the company name to me personally." She sipped her margarita. "Anyway, the import thing is way more advanced than just an idea. I still have all the contacts from when Roger and I lived in Indonesia. And I did that trial run last year, remember? Everything I brought over sold right away. Those painted blinds? They were gone within a month."

"I love that bedspread you guys made me."

"Oh my god, Dani, the fabrics are so cheap. Sam's been great. He's got so many ideas about cushions, drapes, and table runners. No one is doing what we are doing, combining Indonesian textiles with Western design. But I need to be buying and shipping in bigger quantities to get the economics to work out."

"Well, it sounds like your meeting went well."

"Not exactly. The numbers are all good, but the guy wouldn't even look at them. He's like all 'Thank you, Ms. umm-Brook' but I really just can't be bothered."

Danielle twirled her glass around. Nothing but ice left. "Well, that's ridiculous. The guy can't even look at a sheet of paper?" She set her glass on the table and looked around for a waiter.

"Dani, you're in the business. Three years of accounts are more than a page!"

"Oh god, Brook. Let me get you another drink." Danielle caught the waiter's eye and raised two fingers. "Don't tell me 'little Miss Brook' walked in there with her whole bloody filing cabinet!"

Brook looked away.

"Brook, this is what I'm good at," said Danielle. "Even if my bosses don't know it. Let's get you some summary sheets. Nice and simple charts and graphs. So you can whiz in there next time looking like a pro and knock their socks off in mere minutes."

"Thanks Dani. That would help."

Two new margaritas landed on the table. "Cheers," said Brook, reaching for her menu. "I guess we should think about ordering some food. Oh and hey – I've been meaning to ask – how's your brother?"

"Oh my god." Danielle reached for her phone. "He called today. I forgot to call him back ... He's been doing way better."

"I haven't seen Max in ages," said Brook.

"Well, he's got a show this weekend, a big one. I think that's what he's calling about. Feel like going?"

Max strutted down stage left and whirled. From their front-row seats, Brook could see the glittering beads of sweat fly off his brow. He stopped suddenly and crouched, the microphone held high, his hair falling in damp tendrils across his face. It seemed he was singing right at her. The crowd screamed. To her own surprise, Brook screamed too.

After the show, Brook and Danielle waited for Max in a booth at the bar across the street.

"Nicer here, hey? Where we can actually hear one another?" said Danielle. She looked down at her phone. "He says he'll be here in ten."

"I can't believe how much he's changed! His new look ... it's totally working!"

"Oh, that god-awful hair," said Danielle. "Mom and Dad were so concerned. So was I. He's been through some tough times this past year. Drinking. Other stuff too, I think. Not caring for himself."

"Danielle, he looks fantastic!"

Danielle peered into her gin and tonic and gave it a swirl. "Maybe on stage. I just think that that long hair, getting all skinny and that – I don't think it's any planned new look. He just wasn't taking care of himself. Mom and I went over one time. He was a mess."

"But Danielle – look at him tonight! You've got to admit that he's really good with this new stuff."

"Brook, it's the same music he's been flogging for years! It's just louder now." She put her glass down. "But yeah, I agree, it was okay."

Just then, a tray of drinks appeared on the table and Max slid into the seat beside Brook. "Good evening, ladies. G&Ts I presume?" He passed the drinks around.

"Hey bro, great show," said Danielle.

"Hey Max, haven't seen you for ages," said Brook. "That was great. Wow, I don't know what to say. You've changed so much."

"Thanks," said Max. "Yeah, it's been amazing these last few weeks."

"I saw the spread in the paper," said Brook. "Great write-up. I'm so glad you're getting the success you deserve, after so much hard work."

"Well, that's the weird part," Max replied. "I *was* working so hard at this. Not just me, the whole band, for so many years. But last year I just ... well, I guess I gave up."

Danielle and Brook's eyes met.

"Don't know how much Dan has told you," he continued, then looked up at Danielle. "I'm okay talking about it now, Dan."

He turned back to Brook. "I went through a bit of a rough patch. Got into some things I probably shouldn't have." He paused and swirled his drink. "Missed a few rehearsals and the guys got pissed off. Like I said, I got into some things ... I used to be so on it, calling around, basically working my butt off to get us gigs. But I just wasn't into it anymore."

"So what changed?" asked Brook.

"I don't know. That's what I mean; it was weird. I know my family was worried. Eric too." He turned to Danielle. "Remember when you and Mom came over?"

She nodded.

"And the guys were threatening me. Then Steve quit, and Eric almost did too." He looked down. "I think I need a beer." He signalled to a server.

The beer arrived and Max took a swig. "So I started trying to pull things together. Turned my phone back on. I hadn't returned any calls for, like, months. And there were all these messages – promoters asking me to return their calls. It was like, I could never get them to call me back, and all of a sudden they're all calling me. Begging me!"

Danielle leaned in. "It was all those years of hard work, Max. Finally paying off."

"I don't think so, Dan. Sure, hard work made me the musician I am. But it was something else. I wasn't eating well, wasn't shaving, or even cutting my hair. Somehow, all that gave me the 'right look'. And me not calling those guys back..." He paused. "It made them want me. More."

"Well, whatever it is, I'm glad things are going better for you," said Danielle. "But I do think you should cut that hair."

Max snorted. "I want to. Ray won't let me."

Danielle rolled her eyes. "Bloody Ray! What does he know?"

"He got me that gig," Max said. "And an even bigger one tomorrow night." But Max didn't sound so convinced. Then he paused and looked up. Danielle and Brook followed his gaze.

Two girls were standing at the table. The dark-haired one in front spoke first. "We loved the show. You were great!"

"Oh my god!" exclaimed the shorter one. "It was *so* good!"

"Would you..." said the first one, holding out a CD.

"Sure," said Max, and he whipped out a pen so quickly it seemed he had been expecting them. "What's your name?"

He signed the CD with a flourish and thanked them. But the two girls stayed.

"Umm, there's a party tonight," said the first one, handing him a slip of paper. "Maybe see you there?"

Max smiled and accepted the paper. The girls waited awkwardly a moment then the short one tugged at the other one's arm and they slipped away.

"Whoa!" exclaimed Danielle in mock surprise. "My brother's a big celebrity!"

"Shut up, Dan," said Max.

"But Max," Brook said, "that's great! You've got your pick of the girls. That must feel good."

Max's voice suddenly had a hard edge to it. "Maybe I don't want my pick of girls. They don't even know me! Remember when Sandra dumped me last year and wouldn't return my calls? Well, suddenly she's calling me. And Kylie too; we haven't spoken in years! What do they want all of a sudden?

38

Suddenly, I have this hit song and they see me in the papers and hear me on the radio. Now they're interested?"

Max's reaction caught Brook and Danielle by surprise. The trio sipped their drinks in silence.

Danielle said softly, "I always liked Kylie. How is she?"

Max leaned back. "She's good." He put down his beer. "Yeah, I always liked her too."

You remember the story of the Wizard of Oz, right? Dorothy found herself accidentally transported to the mythical Land of Oz by a tornado. She desperately wanted to get back home, so she set out on a journey to find the one and only person who might be able to help her: the great and powerful Wizard of Oz. But it turned out the wizard was a fraud. He was just this little guy behind a screen manipulating controls – all smokescreen and mirrors – projecting an image of greatness and power to inspire reverence and awe in his subjects.

The "wizard" had no special powers at all. However, that guy was a master of perception.

Sure, the Wizard of Oz was a fake. And we're definitely not saying that you should lie, or present an untruthful version of yourself, like he did. If you do, it *will* eventually catch up with you. Although it's important to work to actively influence others' perception of you, you must only do that within the context of remaining genuine and true to yourself. You must remain grounded in reality.

However, you can use perception to influence reality, or even to create a new reality – **your own reality**.

Changing perception to changing reality

Unlike that fraudulent wizard, if you can be truthful and genuine while using the strategies of perception, you can change your own reality for **real**. Let's look a bit deeper into this.

Perception is not the same as reality, but perception creates reality. Like the example we gave earlier, someone might think you are untrustworthy because you are shy and have trouble making eye contact. That doesn't suddenly make you untrustworthy. But if others perceive you that way, it will hold you back in real life.

Let's say, however, that you realize your shyness is causing you to lose opportunities. You make a decision to overcome it. You work more on speaking up, smiling, and on making and maintaining eye contact. People now don't automatically come to the conclusion that there is something shady about you – and more doors might open up for you.

> **By changing their perception,**
> **you've changed your reality!**

Perception can change reality for better or for worse. Look at Max; it's done both for him. He went through his "rough patch," and as a result he picked up a different type of fan and became more in demand. It was good for his career. But it was not a change he wanted, and he doesn't seem to be happy in his new reality because it's not in line with who he truly is.

You can also change your own reality by finding alternatives to how you perceive things yourself: Is it possible to see a situation in another light, and maybe even find some opportunity there? For example, some people might perceive an economic downturn as the worst time to start a new business. But for others, it's perceived as a time of change and new doors opening – perhaps a great time to start something new.

The real deal

Just to highlight something crucial: We are talking about changing perception to create a different, and more favorable, reality for yourself. That is not the same thing as being deceptive or pretending that reality is something it is not.

As you go through this book, you will see that we talk a lot about how you can influence other people's perception of you (and, just a reminder, by "you" we include your business, your brand, your products, your services, and your ideas). But before you get to work on that gentle art of influencing, you will have to decide what perception you **want** them to have. We will get into that in a lot more detail in the next chapter.

Remember, being genuine is super-important! People are not dumb; they see through insincerity or pretense. You want to make sure the perception that you are trying to create of yourself really does reflect your true self, not some made-up image that you can't hold up. This is a big mistake a lot of people make. They realize they need to change their image, but they come up with something uber-fancy or unrealistic that they can't maintain. It might work for a short period of time, but it will eventually backfire, just like it did for the wizard.

You can, however, find a balance between being genuine about who you are now and **who you want to become**. That's the influencing-reality part of changing perception: Changing the perception of how you are seen, whether by yourself or others, can work to help you change yourself. Just make sure that you never disregard who you truly are in your core. Use perception to find your own genuineness, not to mask it. This may take some time and deeper work, but it is very well worth it.

Being genuine is just as important when marketing your brand or services or products. You want to give out the perception that what you offer is quality and reliability. But even before that, you must make sure that what you offer really **is** high-quality and reliable. False claims will come back to bite you on the butt!

The dairy giant Dannon got in trouble for trying to create a false perception. In its advertising, Dannon claimed that its yogurts and other products were "clinically proven" to do everything from improving bowel regularity to preventing cold and flu. In addition to all of the bad press they received as a result of the false claims and resulting scandal, Dannon also had to pay out $45 million in damages to bamboozled consumers and other parties. A very expensive mistake.

Think carefully about the perception you want people to have of you. This should not be any lie or fake image. It must be true to either what you already are or what you want to be and, realistically, can become.

It doesn't matter what type of business you are in – whether you manufacture products, or offer services, or sell ideas – how your brand and your products are perceived has everything to do with the level of success you achieve. The perception people have of you, whether accurate or not, is influencing your reality right now, and it will continue to do so in the future.

If your product is perceived as innovative and cutting-edge, those who are innovators at heart will want to buy it, and they will look to you for new innovations in the future. If your brand is perceived as reliable, more people will naturally come to you when they need something, rather than researching and shopping around. You can use perception to bring across any image.

Going into business requires a plan and action on that plan. Staying in business requires sales. (No, money isn't everything;

but you still have to turn a profit if you want to stay in business or at least cover your costs.) Making sales means that people – the right people, your target market – are coming to you. And they will only do that if they have a good perception of you. There is a lot of choice out there and you need to make sure you are their choice.

Even though perception is one of the most crucial things when building a brand, it is the one that most often gets neglected by business owners. By learning about the importance of perception, you can actively and deliberately manage how you are perceived. You can use perception and brand positioning to create a specific image in your prospect's mind. Perception can be used to influence what opinion the market has of your product or service in comparison to your competitors' products or services.

Managing perception well translates to success.

Going into business is a dream that many with an entrepreneurial spirit have. Unfortunately, many are unable to transform that dream into a reality. However, by using the techniques of perception, you can create your own reality. If there is a market for what you have to offer, perception can help transform your dreams into success.

How you are perceived right now

You may not have even thought of how others perceive you. How do you know what they think?

Brook might feel that she is a really good businesswoman, with a successful company and great plans for expansion. And she might even **be** an amazing businesswoman. But when she flies into the bank manager's office, breathless and frazzled with a big disorganized stack of papers, is the bank manager going to perceive her that way? Not likely.

The best way to find out how others perceive you is to ask. This can be a very scary exercise because you never know whether what you are going to hear is what you **want** to hear. You may be pleasantly surprised (most of us are so insecure, and always fear that people think lower of us than they really do). But you may hear some things that are also difficult to accept. If so, don't take them as criticism; take them as a launching point.

Ask and you shall receive

Start with a trusted friend or a valued client. Ask them what they think of you; in particular, what their perception of your strengths and weaknesses are. Additionally, if you have received any professional feedback over the last few years, such as a performance review, a response to a job application, or product reviews (or complaints), go back and take a look at that. List all the pros and cons. Now, how does what others think of you align with how you perceive yourself? Were there any points that were surprising to you, or disappointing?

The next step is to define how you would like to be perceived. Then we will look at all the different things you can do to create the perception that will lead you to the reality and the success you want.

Define How You Want to be Perceived

Joanna was all smiles when Brook came in. "Brook, where have you been?"

"Late night last night, sorry. Anything I have to deal with?"

"Ta-dah!" Joanna sang back, and she held a magazine open for Brook to see. "*Urban Living*! Ten pages!"

"What?" Brook put down her coffee. "Holy! I never thought they would use all those photos!" She flipped through the pages. "Oh my god, a huge honking full feature!"

Joanna was practically dancing. "The *Times* and the *Sun* want to interview you. And the morning show wants a spot too." She handed Brook a stack of pink message slips. "And the Faluccis are ready to sign."

"Wow, I can't believe this," Brook said, flipping through the pages. "I'll take a look at this while I finish my coffee. Tell Sam to come in; I need to talk to him."

Brook was still flipping through the feature when Sam tapped at her door.

"Come on in, Sam, and take a seat."

"Congrats, Brook," he smiled. "And side by side with the feature on Akito Asumi."

"Oh my god, he's my favorite architect! I never thought ... And look, they did your settee design as a double page. This is thanks to you, too, Sam." She turned another page and looked up. "And you know what? I've been thinking ... Your idea has kind of grown on me. The imports business is going to be called 'Savvy Mundo.'"

"Really?" Sam smiled.

"You're right; it does represent what we're trying to do. And it's fun too." She leaned in. "I actually like a lot of your ideas, Sam. I want you to take on more responsibility. I want to turn more of the clients over to you. Without me overseeing."

Sam's face burst into a huge grin.

"I want to put more of my time towards the imports – to Savvy Mundo. And less to the designing, at least for now. I'm going to raise my prices, so we funnel more of the clients away from me and over to you."

"That's great news, Brook," said Sam, still grinning. "I'm all up for it."

"The Falucci project will be all yours. And I want you to work more closely with Ming and Gustavo," Brook continued. "Get them involved in the projects with you; let them in on your process. I want them to learn from you and eventually take on their own projects too. We're growing, and we need to be ready for this. All of us."

"Brook, I'm all with you," Sam said. "Thanks for this opportunity."

Over at Robertson & Kline, Danielle's day was not going as well as Brook's. She was stuck in a meeting with the bosses, both Mister Robertson and Mister Kline, as well as a weasley-looking lawyer.

"We've engaged Cedric as our counsel," said Mr. Robertson, nodding at the lawyer. "Danielle, you're aware of the issues we had with the Hamilton case. I want you to work with Cedric to clean up that mess."

Danielle looked at Cedric. She'd never met a Cedric before, but he looked just how she imagined one would be: the standard pin-striped suit, clean-shaven, hair neatly slicked to one side. *This guy will be a ton of fun to work with. Could you look any blander, Cedric?*

"Yes, Mr. Robertson." She smiled at Cedric. "It will be my pleasure."

Mr. Kline leaned across the table. "And, ah, Danielle?"

Danielle didn't like this tone. "Yes?"

He paused and smiled meaningfully at Cedric.

Cedric caught the hint. "I think you're done with me for now?" Mr. Robertson nodded. Cedric stood up and smiled at Danielle. "I look forward to working with you."

The Misters Robertson and Kline nodded their goodbyes to Cedric then Mr. Kline turned back to Danielle. "I would like you to work on your, ah, style."

Danielle looked down at her suit. It was Ralph Lauren.

"I mean your communication style," Mr. Kline continued. "Communication in general."

"I'm not sure what you mean," said Danielle.

"Rudy, for example. He's always been very open. We've taken on a lot of new employees the last two years and he helped them. Worked with them."

Danielle looked from Mr. Kline to Mr. Robertson. "Well, I know Rudy likes to chat. I've been focusing on my accounts."

But Mr. Robertson was no help to her. Mr. Kline continued. "Rudy has been a truly valuable mentor. He's helped Alex, Susan, and Dimitri find their place here. But Rudy's attention will be elsewhere these next few months. I'd like you to try to, ah ... to try to open up. Not be so concerned about yourself. Help others. We had a new bunch start last month."

"Try to be a mentor to them," Mr. Robertson added.

Danielle stared at her lap. Her face was hot. She thought she had been gaining the bosses' attention as a hard worker while Rudy chatted his days away with the new employees.

But it seemed that the Misters Robertson and Kline didn't see it that way.

Mr. Robertson stood up. "Please give it some thought, Danielle. Thank you."

"That was a good show, Max." Ray paced back and forth in front of Max. "In fact, Max, that was a *great* show!"

Max sat down and started to extract his arms from his leather vest. "I know. But..."

"But what? Kid, you've finally found your voice. Your style. Did you see that crowd? They love you!"

"But Ray..." Max sighed. "It's like I was saying before..."

Ray whirled around and stood over Max. "Max, I don't need to hear this crap. You've been playing average music for average crowds for years. I don't even know why I stuck with you. And now we're finally making it. And you're not happy."

"Ray, this is not *me*. It's not my sound. It's not the kind of music I want to be doing."

Ray stopped his pacing. He turned to face Max. "Kid, this is a business. Sure you can talk your lah-di-dah new age 'I feel, I want' crap. But we're here to sell music. And you finally found the recipe. Speaking of which..."

"Ray, don't even start on Eric again!"

"Eric's gotta go."

"Ray, Eric and I have been playing music together since we were fourteen."

Ray started pacing again. "Lah-di-dah, Max." He put his hands over his ears, head down. "Lah-di-dah, lah-di-dah..."

Max leapt up and intercepted him. Ray leaned in, close, edging his face into Max's. Max could feel his hot breath and the damp smell of stale beer and smokes.

"Don't be doing this, kid," Ray warned. "Don't be doing this."

Perception does not exist anywhere other than in people's heads. This means that perception is never set in stone. It is constantly changing, whether you like it or not. The goal is to make sure *you* are the one taking charge, managing and changing how you are perceived proactively, rather than letting other people determine it for you. Here's how.

Choosing your attributes

You or your business can't be known for everything because people just can't retain that much information in their heads. Your message will be much stronger, and their perception of you will be more memorable, if you focus on just a few key attributes.

Let's take a look at a few automobile brands and the attributes that different manufacturers have focused on to create their positioning in the market. Slogans are just one way, of many, that companies use to project their attributes out to the world. They serve as a good example here.

Carmaker: Jeep

Slogan: The toughest 4-letter word on wheels.

Attributes: Tough. Rugged. Rough around the edges.

Carmaker: BMW

Slogans: Sheer driving pleasure. The ultimate driving machine.

Attributes: Luxury, quality.

Carmaker: Jaguar

Slogans: Born to perform. Unleash a jaguar.

Attributes: Speed, performance, power.

Carmaker: Chevrolet

Slogan: Baseball, hot dogs, apple pie and Chevrolet.

Attributes: Home-grown, familiar.

Carmaker: Nissan

Slogan: Built for the human race.

Attributes: Economical, practical.

See how what each of these companies stands for – or at least want to be seen to stand for – is summarized in two or three words? That small list of attributes defines a very clear perception that each one has worked to create. It is a perception that has been consciously created. Without it, these brands would not be noticed in a sea of carmakers.

Ask yourself, "How do I want to be perceived?" or "How do I want my business to be perceived?" Then select a few key attributes that your business, or your product or service, can project out to the world to exemplify that perception. Always keep those key attributes in mind as you take the steps outlined throughout this book to change perception, and make sure you stay consistent. It is in your power to change the perception of you or your business. Right now, it seems that Max and his manager, Ray, have conflicting ideas about what Max's attributes should be. Max will have some critical decisions to make.

If you're not sure where to start in picking your attributes, do some research. Ask for feedback from your customers – especially your repeat customers. What do they like about your product or service already? What keeps them coming back to you? Those are characteristics that you already have and are working for you.

You can also find out where there are voids in the market. What would people like to see in your industry? What would make them buy from you? These are attributes that you can try to work on or acquire.

If you are not known for anything, people won't remember you. Keep it simple though. If you are trying to be known for too many things, people won't remember you either!

Building your brand personality

When it comes to business, determining how your brand is perceived comes down to establishing a distinctive identity.

What are the differences between you and your competitors? What are your strengths; what are your advantages? In other words, what is your **brand personality**?

Your brand personality encompasses numerous attributes — each of which will attract a certain type of clientele. You must understand who your target audience is (your "right people") in order to define, and then create, the type of personality that will appeal to them. Your brand personality will influence who will come to you; hence, it's important to think about this carefully.

Let's go back to one of the examples shared earlier: some of the major international airlines — Qantas and Virgin Airways. Both companies offer nearly identical services on nearly identical routes but have cultivated distinct brand personalities that make them attractive to different types of people. Qantas offer an image of being conservative, reliable, and safety conscious, whereas Virgin has cultivated a personality of being hip, fun, and edgy. Based on these brand characteristics, they attract a different market segment. It is part of their positioning.

There is no right or wrong brand personality. It is your choice. Do you want to be seen as fun and friendly or as corporate and conservative? Are you cutting edge and a risk-taker or are you established and old-school?

Depending on your business, it may help to make your business brand an extension of your own character; it is not necessary, though.

In defining your brand personality, you must take into account:

- who your target market (your "right people") is and what their values are (We touched on this in *Chapter 1 Why Perception.*)
- which niches are open and begging to be filled
- which brand personality rings true with your own values and personality. You need to be able to consistently implement it across all channels.

Following are some key areas to examine as you work to determine your brand personality.

Your Purpose Statement

If you've been in business for more than a day, you've probably heard about vision, purpose, mission, and values many times before, so we are not going to repeat it all in detail. We like summarizing these into an attractive Purpose Statement that makes sense for you, your team, and your clients.

So here are some things to consider. It helps to think about the four aspects individually first and then combine them into a single Purpose Statement.

Your **VISION** is your big goal for the company – what you want to have achieved in, say, five or twenty years. For example, your vision might be "to transform the lives of one million people."

Your **MISSION** is how you will achieve your vision. For example, it might be "to provide health education through seminars and online courses."

Your **VALUES** are your guiding principles; they are like your compass. What are some of the things you won't compromise on? Some examples could be sustainability, customer experience, or fair trade – or even fun! (That's one of ours.)

Your **PURPOSE** is the answer to "Why am I doing this? What's the purpose?" It can encompass all of the motivations behind the other three aspects: your vision, your mission, and your values. Putting careful thought into your Purpose Statement is an important exercise because it is what makes you attractive to all your stakeholders.

Your look

Your look is the translation of your character into visuals. It encompasses everything from the design of your logo to the colors and fonts you use in your marketing pieces, the décor of your office space, and how you dress. And if what you sell is a physical product, it also includes the design of your packaging and of the products themselves.

Apple is a great example of integrating product design with the overall look of their brand. You can pretty much recognize a product as being from Apple with a quick glance at its design. You don't even need to see their logo.

Think about the brand personality you are aiming for and how you can use your look to help create that perception.

If you want to create the perception that you are traditional and established, you can use classic fonts and conservative colors. But if you want to create the perception that you are innovative and high-energy, you probably will want to gravitate to trendier fonts and color palettes. It's always best to work with an experienced design team as they can help you translate your brand personality into visuals.

Your team

Your team consists of all the people associated with your business: its leaders and team members, and possibly other affiliates such as consultants, or even celebrities who endorse your product.

Your team needs to know how you want your business to be perceived, so they can help you spread that image and ensure consistency. You also want to make sure that whomever you invite to be on your team fits into your brand personality.

Many businesses can benefit hugely from working on how their team is perceived or even just by communicating to the public who their team are. For example, if you are a new local boutique restaurant, letting the public know that the tomatoes were grown down the road by Ed and Judy (your extended team), and that your chef Julio learned to cook in Italy but returned to settle in your town with his wife and young family, suddenly makes your establishment more attractive. Now it's different and it's personal.

Talk to your team members about what your brand personality is, and involve them in the process! This can include anything from guidelines on how they dress to instructions on how they interact with clients. A tradesman might want their team members to all wear neatly branded shirts. A high-end resort might be trying to pamper people with luxury and always be super-formal and polite. An alternative marketing agency might want to catch attention by being edgy, adventurous and fun, and doing outrageous things that their clients remember. (Hey, that's us! Footwear is non-compulsory!)

Your communication

How you communicate also reinforces that brand personality and the overall perception that people have of your business. This includes anything from instructions to your team members on how to interact with the public (super-formal and polite or laid-back, friendly, and remember-your-name) to how the copy is written in the marketing pieces you put out.

We gave the example a while back of the Virgin Airlines website. On their booking page, their copy says "Cheers to a trip. Get out of town with awesome low fares" above a click-here button. That style of communicating would not work for most international airlines, but for Virgin, aiming for the perception of "we're fun, we're who the cool people turn to," it is a perfect fit. Awesome low fares? Click!

Think about your own communication style and be consistent.

Your marketing pieces

Some people think that marketing pieces mean only printed things, like brochures and magazine ads. (And then they think *Whoa, I don't have a budget for that!*) But print ads form only a small part of the range of what we call "marketing pieces."

Your marketing pieces are everything you put out to the world: your website, your social media posts, your logo – even your business name.

Take Brook, for example. She probably didn't think much about where her business might go when she was just starting out, and "Designs by Brook" probably suited it fine for what it was back then. But now she has grown. She has employees and an office and needs to position herself better to the higher-end clientele. Now "Designs by Brook" can still work, but it sounds kind of small-town; a more grown-up name might suit her better.

But please don't think that you have to change your business name to grow a successful business; you absolutely don't! There are countless big brands out there with the weirdest names that prove the opposite!

Your reputation

It's not about what you say anymore; it's about what others say *about you*. It's about how you are being perceived and what they "tweet" to their friends all over social media.

The digital revolution has changed marketing. Your marketing pieces used to be restricted to paid advertising:

magazine or newspaper ads, television commercials, print brochures. The internet, that global web of instantaneous communication, has changed that forever, to the better, as it is easier than ever before for a clever small business to be seen without having to spend millions on marketing.

Getting others to talk about you is not only super-effective, it is free! And it offers a huge difference in credibility. What would you be more likely to believe: a paid advertisement that reads "Our coffee is the best coffee in the world" or your friend telling you, "Oh my god, it was the best coffee I've ever tasted – you would love it!"?

This is one reason that so many brands use celebrity endorsements. Those famous public figures may not be our friends in real life, but we tend to look up to them and respect them, valuing their opinions almost like we do our own friends' – or even more! As irrational as it may sound!

Another way to get people talking about you is to drum up media coverage. Articles about your company or your products hold more weight in consumers' minds than your own paid advertising. A magazine ad saying that your running shoe is the most comfortable shoe you will ever run in does not have the same credibility as an independent gear review article saying the exact same thing. The feature on Brook's designs in *Urban Living* is bound to raise her profile and do far more than any media campaign she pays for herself. Getting great publicity is one of the fastest ways for a business or person to influence their perception (and no, not all publicity is good publicity!).

Get people talking about you! Besides the fact that their opinions are seen as more impartial, and trustworthy, than your own advertising campaign, people tend to pass on things they have heard from friends more. The world of social media, especially social platforms such as Facebook, make sharing recommendations and "liking" products or businesses easier than ever.

Your products and services

So far, we have mainly been talking about your brand. But most of these same points apply to your products or product line, and to the services you offer. Just as for your brand, the first thing to do is to pick the attributes you want your products (we're including services in that) to be known for.

If you offer a number of products, the attributes you choose for them don't have to be exactly the same as the attributes of your brand. For example, you can develop a line of products aimed at different markets, such as your regular line of hand-crafted leather shoes and your "luxury" line, or your basic car-cleaning service and your "premium" service.

The characteristics can be different, but do make sure they are compatible. You can't try to sell your company as the "conservative, traditional, reliable" brand but then advertise products that promote risk or adventure – at least not if you want consumers to have some consistent perception of you.

But What if YOU Are the Product?

That was just too much. The bosses don't think she talks enough at work. And now she's going to have to work with that weasley lawyer. Danielle needed a coffee.

Marie was already at the sink, empty coffee pot in hand. Danielle paused at the door. "Hey Marie," she started, but Marie was in mid-conversation with one of the new guys. With the running water, neither of them heard her. The tone seemed serious. Danielle stepped back. They hadn't noticed her.

"Yeah, my first year here, no one really talked to me either," Marie was saying. "I felt kind of clueless."

"How long have you been here?" Tony asked.

"Three years now," said Marie.

"But what happened. Different people?"

"No," Marie continued. "I didn't even understand how to work a new spreadsheet. But Rudy seemed nice, so I asked him for help. You know who he is?"

"The Accounting Manager?"

"Yeah, that's his new position. He was just a junior accountant back then." Marie switched off the tap and reached up to the cupboard. "Here, hold this."

She passed Tony the coffee pot and opened a package of coffee. Danielle held her breath and glanced up and down the corridor. No one around.

"And it turned out he was super helpful. So after that I just kept asking him for help, even on little things. He was so nice. And I learned a lot. Here, pass me that." She nudged the coffee pot into the machine and flicked the switch. "And I got a lot better at my job."

"So Rudy's the one I should get to know?"

"Well, he's manager now. He's not going to be that available. But pick someone like him, one of the accountants. A smart one."

"I heard that Danielle is really smart."

"Oh god, Danielle!" Marie threw her head back and turned to Tony. Danielle ducked further back into the hallway. "Yeah, she probably is smart. But she is *so* stuck up. She struts around in her Dior whatever – barely can stoop to say a word to anyone."

Danielle put her hand to her mouth. She held her breath.

"No, someone smart but friendly. Like Helen maybe. Or Dimitri. He's more junior but he is hilarious – really nice guy."

Danielle backed silently down the hallway. Her head was pounding. She was desperate for a coffee, but there was no way she was going back to that room.

"Thanks for coming over, Dani," said Max.

"No probs. I need some friendly face-time with my bro anyway," she said. "And I want to see that new guitar that you can't stop talking about!"

Max opened the guitar case on the table and picked the instrument up gingerly. "Here she is."

"It's acoustic," Danielle said, surprised. "When will you ever use that?"

"She's beautiful," Max said. He sat down on a speaker and strummed it, then fiddled with the tuning. "You want to hear my newest song?"

Danielle stretched out on the floor as Max started to play – a slow and sad ballad. When he was done, she asked, "But when will you ever use it? I mean, the song is beautiful, more like your old stuff. But it doesn't fit where you are now. What does Ray think?"

"Bloody Ray," said Max. He set the guitar on a stand and joined Danielle on the floor. "Ray wants me to ditch Eric."

"What?"

"Yeah. Like we've been together since we were kids."

"Eric's written half the songs! And he's the most 'brilliantest' keyboard player we've ever known," Danielle exclaimed.

"I know! But Ray says Eric's sound doesn't fit what I'm doing."

"Fit what?" said Danielle. She extended her leg and hunched forward. "Sorry, I need to stretch. Brook and I went for a run this morning, my first one in two months. I had to work to keep up with her. Anyway, Eric's a perfect fit for what you just played me."

"Ray says I need to think of it as a business. He says we finally found the 'recipe'. But to me it's more pure than that. It's my art."

"Bro," said Danielle, "it is a business too. What else do you have to live off?"

"Producing! Dan, I don't even like being on stage any more. At least not this long-haired rock star stuff. Sure it makes me money." He snorted. "Some, after Ray gets his 25%. But I've produced both of our albums, and I know what I'm doing there."

"You mean you want to be a producer?"

"Dan, I've been doing that for years already! Remember Talking Eyes and Jailhouse, and Sarah J? Sure, they never made me millions, but they got great reviews. And look where Sarah went to after that." He gazed down at the new guitar.

"But Max," Danielle said, "you're an amazing musician."

"But I can still do that. My own way. Small venues, quieter stuff – just Eric and me. Meaningful stuff. Like we used to play."

Danielle sat up. "Can you make a living off that?"

"The producing?" Max asked. "Yeah, you can make good money as a producer. And I could play gigs on weekends too, for fun. I don't need a lot."

"I think you should follow your heart. I didn't think this whole 'look' thing was really you anyway. And now hearing what you're saying..." She looked him in the eye. "Don't ditch Eric. Ditch Ray."

"That's my big sis! She gets it." Max smiled. "You want a beer? Or a coffee?"

"No, I'm good thanks." She switched her stretch to her other leg.

"What about you?" Max asked. "Anything new and amazing in your life?"

"Oh my god, they've got this new lawyer. One of the many things that sucks with my job right now. Actually, I will have a beer if you have any."

"This is a studio!" Max chuckled. "Of course I have beer!" He reached over to the bar fridge.

"One of our clients is suing us, and I have to work with this guy on it," Danielle continued.

"Yuck, lawyers," said Max. "Pretty nasty?"

"Nasty's not exactly the word," said Danielle. "Pass me the opener? No, just non-descript. A plain nerdy kind of guy. Probably harmless. Amazing he made it to be a lawyer, really."

"Well, harmless is okay, isn't it?"

"No, Max, you wouldn't believe it! He asked me if I wanted to go to some show with him next weekend!"

"What did you say?"

"I didn't say anything; I was kind of floored."

"On Saturday? I'm going to a show on Saturday. Some friends of Eric's; they're really good. Why don't you come? I was thinking of asking Kylie. And then you can tell this guy you're previously committed."

"You've been talking to Kylie?" Danielle asked, eyebrows raised.

"She's left me a few messages. I haven't called back. But just hearing her voice..."

"I always liked her, Max. I don't get why you guys split up."

"I know," said Max wistfully. "That trip we did to New Zealand..."

"Oh my god," Danielle broke in, giggling. "That so-called backpacking trip, when you guys had like two guitars and a ukulele?"

Max laughed. "And a banjo. And the harmonicas."

"I can *not* imagine traveling like that," said Danielle.

"Dan, that was the best month of my life."

"Well, call her then. And sure, I'll come too. Can I ask Brook and Roger too? So I don't feel like my little brother's chaperone?"

"Thanks sis," said Max. "How does the rest of the world live without your wise words?"

Danielle thought of Marie, and of Tony. *They seem to do just fine, actually*. She took a swig of her beer.

Danielle finished her coffee and set the mug down. She took a deep breath. She didn't like talking to people she didn't know.

But little bro Max seemed to think she was a good mentor. *Here goes...* She jumped up and casually strolled to where her new colleagues were working.

"Hi. You're Tony, right?" She turned to the guy sharing his desk. "Sorry, I don't know your name. I'm Danielle."

The second guy looked up, then stood and held out his hand. "I'm Hatsuo."

Tony stood too. "Hello Danielle. I've heard lots about you."

I know you have, thought Danielle. But all she did was shake Tony's hand and say, "I just wanted to welcome you both." She turned to Hatsuo. "I know it's hard when you're just starting, not knowing your way around or the company yet."

They both looked at her expectantly.

"Umm," she continued. "My office is just over there. Second on the right. I'd be really happy to help. If you need anything."

This isn't going well, she thought.

But then Hatsuo smiled. "Thank you, Danielle. That's really kind of you. I was actually wondering ... Do you have a moment right now, or am I bothering you?" He pointed to his computer screen.

"No, go ahead. What's up?" said Danielle, stepping around the desk so she could see. "Oh sure, the receivables. Here, look. We have this in-house software." She reached for the mouse.

Tony leaned in.

"Here, Tony, can you see? It seems weird at first, but it totally makes sense. Just let me grab a chair." Tony rolled two chairs around to Hatsuo's side of the desk and Danielle sat down to explain.

Some businesses sell a physical product or a service. But in some businesses, **you** are the product. This class of business includes any business where people want you and your product is you. This could be a consultant, hair stylist, interior designer, architect, teacher, dentist, and so on.

Sure, if this is your type of business, there are other people out there who do what you do. But your clients select you because of **you**: your "hard" personal attributes including skills and qualifications, track record and recommendations, and your "softer" attributes, or more emotional reasons – they have a good feeling about you, like your vibe.

When you are the product, how people perceive you is doubly important. You are a business, so all of the tips we gave in the previous chapter about perception and your brand or business apply. You are, however, also a human being. As we noted in the opening chapter, people are constantly forming opinions of one another – whether rightly or wrongly – based upon everything from your appearance to how you speak, how you dress, your body language. The bank manager perceives Brook as disorganized and therefore unprofessional;

Max's new fans perceive him as a wild boy; and Danielle's coworkers perceive her as rude.

Much of anyone's decision to work with you or not comes down to how they perceive you. Whether you like it or not, it is in your best interests to choose how you want to be perceived, and then take the actions to influence and achieve that perception.

Influencing perception

How you dress

We don't want to give the impression that perception is all superficial and we are certainly no fashion gurus. But people **do** judge you on how you look and come to a very quick conclusion – right or wrong – about what kind of person you are. And how you dress is part of that.

It's not so simple that all you have to do is put on a suit and you will get promoted. But clothing is an "identifier", unfortunately.

Here's a little exercise. Take a look at this list. Each item is a very brief description of a man's appearance:

- a man with a full beard, wearing a faded plaid shirt, work pants, and gumboots
- a clean-shaven man with his hair trimmed short, wearing a dark grey suit and dark blue tie

- a man with nose and eyebrow piercings, hair dyed black, dressed in tight leather pants, a black T-shirt, and boots
- a man with his hair combed back into a short pony tail, wearing a plain T-shirt, new jeans, and leather shoes

All we're talking about here are basic details about superficial appearance, yet we'll bet that, in spite of such limited and superficial information (and never actually meeting these hypothetical guys!), you formed some opinions about them. You might even already like some and dislike or even distrust others.

Sounds kind of unfair, right? Judging people based upon their appearance?

Well, it is certainly very superficial, but all of the descriptions listed above are things that those men have chosen (like clothing, hair style) to represent themselves. Those men are sending out a certain message, whether consciously or not. And you received.

So this is why how you dress is actually important. This is why there are dress codes for many careers – even if those codes are merely understood, not written.

Look at Brook and Danielle: both women with a love for fashion and a great dress sense. Each travel in completely different professional worlds.

Brook is a designer and her fashionable dress sense helps augment her reputation as artistic, trendy, and current. Danielle, on the other hand, works in a conservative accounting office. Showing up to work wearing the latest fashions doesn't give the perception that she is practical or responsible with money; in fact, it might lead to the opposite perception.

This doesn't mean that Danielle should give up on her passion for fashion. It just means that she should not amplify that part of her character at work. When she goes to work, she needs to dress for the part – still in line with herself but maybe a bit more toned down.

How you behave

There is a concept that we will explore more deeply in our bonus chapter (*Chapter 10 Perception in Your Personal Life*) that we call "internal perception." Most of this book focuses on "external perception"– how the world outside sees you. Internal perception is how you see yourself.

If you have a poor perception of yourself, or a low self-image, this will come across to others – both in terms of how you run your business and in your own body language and behavior. If you keep behaving and speaking as if you are not very good, that attitude is going to rub off on others. You will influence how they perceive you and they may start believing that about you as well. However, if you behave in a confident manner, as if you believe in yourself and your products, others will catch on. By thinking about and working on your own internal perception, you will also influence others' perception of you.

Most of us automatically adjust our behaviors according to who we are with and who we want to impress (if anyone).

For example, at a casual dinner with old friends from high school, Fred might talk with his mouth full and reach across the table for a plate of food, without a second thought. But the next night, at a corporate dinner with the new CEO from out of town, Fred's natural behavior would likely be different: speaking in full sentences (and swallowing first!) and asking if James would please pass the peas (if he even goes for seconds at all).

Much of our behavior comes naturally. The key here is to become more conscious of it. Think carefully about any gathering, whether it is some special social or work event, or whether it is just your day-to-day social interactions in the office. Danielle felt she was giving the perception that she was hard-working and focused by not chatting much at work. To her dismay, though, she's found out that her colleagues' perception of her is that she is unfriendly and a snob.

Think about how you speak and the words you use and the messages you convey through your behavior and body language. Make sure that the messages you are giving are consistent with the perception you want others to have of you.

Your track record

Your track record speaks massively about who you are and whether or not you are the "real deal." Your track record is the accumulation of your accomplishments. In the business world, these would be any awards or prizes your business or products have won, any media exposure, testimonials, reviews and other ways of listing your successes. For example, an architect might have a wall of framed photos of completed projects. A hair stylist might have a photo book of his best feature haircuts.

Your professional track record will include the types of things you would put on a personal CV, such as your academic achievements and your work experience but may also include items more to do with your character such as the friendships you maintain, how supportive you have been to friends in need, your athletic achievements, or your artistic accomplishments.

In the personal world, your track record is a bit different, and it will vary according to who your audience is and what they value. Different aspects of your personal track record will be of interest to different types of people. For example, someone who is interested in you for a potential romantic relationship might want to check out your track record in personal relationships: whether you get along with your parents or have good relationships with your ex-partners. Whereas if you are looking to get invited to be part of a new running group, those people will probably want to know how fast you run and what races you've completed.

Positioning yourself as an authority

Most people respect an authority or expert! Not someone who simply proclaims themselves to be an expert, but someone who truly does have the knowledge and the experience – the "real deal."

In the business world, being recognized as an expert gives the perception of quality, so your clients have confidence in your products or services. Even in your personal life, positioning yourself as an expert will help you win professional recognition and lead to more career opportunities such as job offers or promotion.

But always remember the part about being genuine! It's not about **pretending** to be an expert; it's about becoming one – and letting people know that. Here are some tips for how to do that.

Continuous growth

No matter how expert you may become, no one ever knows everything there is to know. It's impossible! Stay forever on your learning journey; never stop growing. In fact, 'continuous growth' is one of humans' most desired needs. Find instructional videos, research your topics, read books. Try to find time to take courses or attend workshops, whether in person (the advantage here is also networking and making contacts) or online. Opportunities abound.

Talking the talk and walking the walk

Many so-called experts teach a subject, but they do not actually *do* the things they teach themselves. As an example, Jen, who proclaims herself as an expert in raw foods, is a coach and health advisor. Her business is based on the idea that a purely raw foods diet is essential for top athletic performance and overall health.

But when one of her clients caught her at the supermarket with a grocery cart full of canned foods (and no, it wasn't to feed her cat!), Jen's status as an expert dropped immediately. Not only with **that** client, but in the whole community because, of course, word got around! Jen was great at talking her talk, but she wasn't walking the walk.

The same goes for when you see a personal trainer smoking outside the gym or a business consultant struggling to manage her own business. Or a professor who has never run a business talking about entrepreneurship. Talking the talk becomes meaningless if you cannot also walk the walk.

Sharing your knowledge

It may seem wise to hold in your knowledge, keeping all of that valuable information to yourself. You might feel that if you share your knowledge, other people will use it too and you won't be seen as that one expert any more.

But the fact is, there are many reasons to share your knowledge. The first is that when you share, people see you as generous. You are positioning yourself as a giving person, and they feel good about you. Second, if you are generous with your knowledge, people will follow you – even those in your own industry. Trust that they will know where that information and knowledge is coming from, and that you are the source. And finally, how will people ever know that you are the expert if you keep all of your information locked up?

Sharing information is one of the fastest ways to build relationships and gain trust and loyal fans.

This is what Danielle has finally decided to do. By mentoring the new employees, she not only becomes perceived as friendly, generous, and knowledgeable by her colleagues, her bosses are sure to notice, too. And they will begin to perceive her as being more valuable.

Getting out there

Get out there! Making contacts and networking are important, and they are opportunities for you to be seen as an active participant in your industry or community. Even better is if you can get out there in some sort of leadership role: teaching a course, or as a guest speaker, or being head of a committee. Join associations and clubs, participate in governing bodies, attend meetings, join forums, and participate in conversations – both online and offline. Make sure you are both seen and heard.

Becoming "talkaboutable"

What people say about you carries a special believability that cannot be found in your planned and scripted marketing pieces.

How do you get others to talk about you? Being great makes people talk about you, so follow the steps above and share your awesomeness. (Yes, you are trying to be *perceived* as an authority in your field, but remember the part about being genuine: You have to walk the walk and actually **be** that expert too). Be the best you can be at what you do. So people want to talk about you. Being generous also makes people talk about you. You can do this by sharing information and resources, or perhaps offering a link to a free video training or a short online course for free.

And of course, you can always ask your satisfied clients to "tell their friends." But, in reality, they will only do this if you have impressed them. So work on being the best you can be, be generous, be different (more on that in the next chapter) and you will become "talkaboutable".

Think Differentiation

"**S**am, I just don't see that there will be a market for that." Brook was trying to be open-minded. Sam had a very different way of thinking and some of his ideas had turned out great. But this was just getting weird. "How many people would ever buy one?"

"Square cushions are boring," Sam continued. "Round ones too. No one is going to pay our kind of prices for them when you can get them at any discount store for a few dollars."

"But all these shapes and those crazy trims, they're..." Brook struggled for a way to phrase it nicely.

"They're different," Sam said.

Brook sighed. "That they are..."

"Brook." Sam turned away from the computer screen and gazed at her earnestly. "I'm not saying we'll sell thousands of them. And we don't want to, anyway. This isn't WalMart; it's Savvy Mundo."

Brook sighed again. "But I just don't think we'll sell very many of them."

"Brook!" Sam exclaimed, finally raising his voice. "We don't *want* to sell many of them! Think exclusive. Think unique. That's why we can be expensive."

Brook was coming around to what he was saying. Sam continued, "Yes, it's a small market. But it'll be all ours!"

Brook's phone buzzed. It was Joanna. "I have a Mr. Vogel on the line?"

"Oh god, it's the bank," Brook replied. "Put him through." Sam gave her a quick encouraging smile and ducked out of her office.

Brook inhaled. She heard the call click through. "Hello Mr. Gr... Vogel!" (*Whoops*) She tried to sound positive. No, more than that.

"Ms. umm, Madame. I've reviewed your file and I'm afraid that we cannot justify a loan of that magnitude. We are going..."

"Mr. Vogel, please!" *Oh god Brook, what are you doing? Don't beg.* "Please. You didn't review my file; you haven't looked at my numbers. The costs on the Indonesia end are so low, it can't help but turn a profit..."

"Madame!"

"There's practically no risk at all! I've gone over..."

"Madame! Brook! Please!"

Brook stopped. She closed her eyes.

"I'm very sorry," Mr. Vogel continued. "We do our very best for our clients, and this is what we believe is in your best interests."

Brook held her breath. What else was there to say?

"You are welcome to try another lending institution. Or perhaps consider a private investor. Thank you for contacting Central Financial."

If he wasn't so scared, Max could almost have taken pleasure in seeing the red creep up from Ray's neck. It spread across his cheeks and over his brow. This *felt* like the right thing to do. But what if Ray was right? Was he committing career suicide?

Ray was trembling. "So what you're telling me is, now that we've made it, you don't want to play music anymore?" Max had never seen him this angry.

"Not like this, Ray," he said. "I'm going to keep playing music, but it's going to be my music. My way." He suddenly had a vision of himself and Eric playing in a quiet corner of the Salamanca.

"You and that dumb-ass are not going to make it. Look at the crowds I got you! We could fill your whole next year with gigs if you stopped being so stupid."

Max didn't know what this next year might bring. But he knew that a year of pretending to be the rock-and-roll persona Ray wanted him to be was *not* on the cards.

Ray was still talking. "... and besides, there's no market for that crap." He was pacing again. He turned on his heel. "What was your 'big' crowd before you had me? Thirty people?"

It was actually eighty. But Max didn't bother to argue. Ray was right about that. His latest gigs with Ray had all drawn over a thousand. "I'll figure it out," Max said.

"Kid, in a couple of months you are going to be begging at my door. And I don't know that I'm gonna have time for you." He whirled around and pushed his way out the door, his voice echoing down the hallway. "Good luck!"

The bell rang. Brook shouted out, "Roger, can you get it? It's probably Danielle."

Roger opened the door and took Danielle's coat. "Hey Danielle. Brook didn't say you were coming. You here for dinner?"

"She just called me. She's got a meeting with another bank tomorrow; they called her last minute. I promised to help her get the paperwork together."

Brook walked in and gave Danielle a hug. "Sorry, I just got home. Didn't even have a chance to tell Roger you were coming."

"Are you staying for dinner?" Roger asked.

"I know it's my turn to cook, sweetie," said Brook. "I thought I'd order Chinese."

"When is your meeting?" asked Roger.

"Tomorrow at ten," answered Brook. "Dani's going to help me prepare."

"Chinese is fine with me," said Roger. "Shout when you're nearly done. I'll call it in."

Brook and Danielle retired to the office. Brook pulled up the past three years of accounts for Designs by Brook, as well as the projections for the import business. "We're going with Sam's name, Savvy Mundo," she said.

"Excellent name!" Danielle grinned. "Smart! And global!"

"I know. It was such a risk committing to take on Sam. But he's been so worth it."

"I hope the others work out for you too. Ming? And who's the other?"

"Gustavo. They're not as outgoing as Sam." She opened the top folder. "But he wasn't either, the first year. I won't have as much one-on-one time with them as I did with Sam. But I think they're going to work out. They each have their own unique presence. Anyway, here are the numbers for Indonesia."

Danielle looked at the top sheet then flipped to the next one "So I don't get what the plan is."

"Two companies," said Brook. "Designs by Brook, with Sam leading. And Savvy Mundo for the imports. I can put more time into it, now with Sam leading Designs by Brook."

Danielle was silent.

"What?" asked Brook.

"So you mean it's like 'Designs by Brook by Sam'? I don't think that's going to go over."

Brook snickered. "I'm kind of jealous of Gustavo. I wish I could be 'Designs by Gustavo'. It sounds so exotic. But he's like twenty-four. He only graduated last year!"

"But Brook, you have a great name," said Danielle. "It's like Gucci or St. Laurent or whoever. It's not like we really believe that those exact guys designed our clothes – some of them are even dead! – but it still gives this feeling of quality, as if they are overseeing the design."

Brook cocked her head, thinking.

Danielle continued. "Designs by Brook sounds hokey. Sorry. But it does. Think about it. You have a **great** name! Use it! How about ... 'Brooklyn Winston Design'?"

"Hmmmm, I guess it does sounds more grown up," said Brook. "It's the same, but totally different I agree ... reminds me a little of when I got in trouble as a kid"

"Hah, I know! You get it, though? Like you are the overseer. You are the Gucci. Brooklyn Winston Design."

"Dani, you're brilliant; you might be onto something here," Brook said. "You are the design queen! Not the typical accountant at all!"

Danielle recalled Marie's "Dior, whatever" comment. She relayed to Brook what she had overheard in the coffee room.

"I had no idea they thought that about me. So I'm trying to fix that," Danielle added. "I went up to two of the new guys this morning and offered to, well, pretty much mentor them. I think it went well."

"Don't worry about what Marie says, Dani," Brook said. "I mean, don't get me wrong, it's true you don't look like an accountant. But that's because you look fabulous! That Marie is just jealous."

Defining differentiation

What you make or do is a commodity. **How** you do it can differentiate you. Your unique way of doing things is part of your **differentiation**.

The purpose of differentiation is to get noticed or to be distinguished from the rest. We'll talk about specific strategies of how to differentiate in Chapter 6. For now, let's look at examples of differentiation.

Let's take some basic commodities like water, salt, or coffee. These commodities are available under numerous brand names, and for the most part they are quite inexpensive. (In most of the developed world, clean drinking water is nearly free, flowing from your tap!) Yet we are willing to pay a premium price once those commodities are differentiated – giving us the perception that they are worth more, and somehow better. Whether that "betterness" is real, or just how we feel about them, is an open question.

That's why many manufacturers of bottled waters are able to sell their water at higher prices than we pay for gasoline for our cars – and look how much we complain about gas prices! That's also why we are willing to pay even three times more for high-end brands of coffee than the lower-end brands such as Nabob and Folgers.

These examples illustrate how basic commodities can be transformed into differentiated products simply by adding an aspect of your company's uniqueness to it.

Why differentiate – and how?

Differentiating can help you carve out a specific market or allow you to charge a higher price. Or both. If you don't want to compete on price (which most don't), you must differentiate. In fact, you **have to** differentiate if you don't want to blend in and go unnoticed.

To differentiate, start by looking at what makes you different – or what **could** make you different. This applies to anything: a person, a business, a product, a service.

Brook runs an interior design business (that's the "what," the commodity). Lots of other people run interior design businesses too. She really needs to think of ways to differentiate, so she can stand out from the rest. Here are a few things she could look at:

- how she runs the business
- her personal touches
- the customer experience
- her location
- her team
- her unique past, having lived in Indonesia, which now places her in the distinct position of coming from two

cultures and being able to blend Indonesian products with Western style in a new and innovative way.

The Differentiation Spectrum

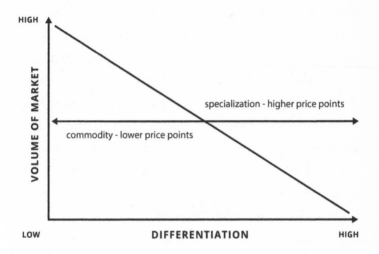

In general, the more differentiation you have, the better – although that may depend somewhat on your industry. If you are in a very crowded space, it helps to become more differentiated, as long as you don't get so narrow or specific that there is no longer a market for you.

The Differentiation Spectrum is a visual of how differentiated your product (or your service or your brand) is. On the left are non-differentiated commodities where you are just one of the crowd. And on the right are differentiated products where you stand out in all your glory! You want to be somewhere between the middle and the far right of the spectrum – if you are not selling a commodity, that is.

Let's look at some examples of undifferentiated products.

What about double-A batteries for your flashlight? We're sure there are a few brand names you've heard of out there, but most likely your purchase decision will be based more on price than on differentiation. Not to say that you can't differentiate batteries.

In most cases, you don't want to be perceived as just a commodity. The further left you go on the Differentiation Spectrum, the more general your market will be. The further right you go, the more differentiated and more specific you become. Your total market may be smaller, but you are more likely to acquire some very loyal fans, early adopters, and come to dominate that smaller pool. You want to be a big fish in a small pond rather than a small, unknown fish in a big pond.

Sam gets this. Brook is nervous about his crazy cushion designs – that there won't be much of a market for them. But Sam is right; Brook doesn't **need** much of a market. She just needs to reach enough of those "right people": the ones who don't want a standard department store cushion; the ones who will be proud to display a unique, exclusive – and expensive – Savvy Mundo cushion on their couch. Many business owners are scared to go to the right because they think they are missing out on business, when in fact they are attracting their perfect market by becoming more irresistible to them.

You need to look at what your possible markets could be and what you have to offer that gets them excited. It might also be smart to look at what your competitors are doing. If all you do is copy them but offer your products cheaper, then you are competing based on price (being more of a commodity, with low differentiation) – and that's hardly ever a good game-plan. But if you can differentiate yourself more, by offering an incredible customer experience, differentiating your products, or by finding a specific niche and gaining loyal fans, then you can position yourself on the right end of the Differentiation Spectrum. Instead of competing on price, you become "talkaboutable", special, desirable – and people will be happy to pay more for your product given that the value outweighs the price.

In general, only very large businesses or business partnerships (those that can compete on price via the economies of scale to become the big discount providers) can succeed on the low-differentiation commodity side of the spectrum. Walmart's positioning, for example, is to be on the very left of the differentiation spectrum, always finding the cheapest products for its customers thanks to buying in bulk. Most small businesses **must** differentiate to survive and thrive. They don't have the advantage of economies of scale and will never be able to compete with the big companies on price and they really shouldn't either. It's a lot more fun to play on the right side of the spectrum!

You call the shots

It's really important that **you** are the one who takes charge of how your brand and products are perceived – how your "right people" recognize your differentiated product or service as the irresistible solution they need. Not being seen at all may be an option in your private life. But it's not an option in business if you want to increase your impact.

If people have heard of you at all, they will have formed some sort of perception of you. Do you want that perception to be created by the market or – even worse – by your competitors? Of course not!

So it's really important to remember that you are the one who should be calling all the shots on how you are perceived. This means:

1. choosing what attributes you want to be known for
2. defining how you want your brand and products to be perceived
3. differentiating i.e. figuring out where you want to position yourself on the Differentiation Spectrum
4. putting yourself out there! ... Our next chapter explains how to do that.

How to Differentiate

D ew glistened on the pine boughs. The pavement was still wet from the previous night's rain.

Danielle was breathing heavily. "I'm glad you got me back into running. I was turning into a slug."

"We're so lucky to have this park," said Brook. She glanced at her watch. "My meeting's at ten. We should probably turn around soon."

"You nervous?" Danielle asked.

"Well, yeah," said Brook.

"Just go in there like you own the place. You deserve this loan, Brook. So act like it, like you deserve it!" She was puffing. "Can we take a little walking break?"

"Sure," said Brook, and they settled into a power-walk.

"Does Roger have a briefcase?" Danielle asked.

Brook nodded. She was puffing, too.

"Why don't you borrow it?" said Danielle. "Put all those extra files in, so it looks full. Leave the summaries on the top. Only show him those summary pages."

"I like my bag," said Brook. "It was super expensive."

"Just use the briefcase, Brook. Play their game — look the part."

Later that morning, in a stylish but conservative suit and with briefcase in hand, Brook tried to keep Danielle's advice in mind. She strode into the bank manager's office. *Like I own the place.*

"Brooklyn Winston," she said, extending her hand. "Pleased to meet you." She snapped the briefcase open, laid the two summary pages on the desk and sat down.

Max looked worried as Kylie struggled for a hand-hold. He called down, "The trail's a bit rougher than last time I was here. Do you need a hand?" She tested a rock then grasped a root and pulled herself up.

"No, I'm good," Kylie laughed as she heaved herself to the top of the outcrop. "What a view!"

The valley extended far below them — forested slopes broken up by a patchwork of small farms, and the river snaking through the middle of it all. It was a stunning day.

Max thought about taking Kylie's hand. "I haven't been up here for years," he said.

She looked up at him. "That's weird. I always imagined that you were doing all of these amazing hikes without me this whole time."

"No..." he said, and his voice trailed off.

"What?" Kylie asked softly.

"I don't know. I kind of lost myself. My values." He looked in her eyes. "I guess I haven't really been very happy these last few years. But I don't think I realized it until now."

She took his hand. "You did kind of lose yourself that last year we were together. But it feels like now you're back. Like when things were good between us. Remember our New Zealand trip?"

"I can't forget that," he said. "That was the happiest time of my life."

"Me too. We should go back some time. Maybe you'll have more time to travel now." She looked up at him. "I mean fun-travel."

Max didn't answer. Kylie saw the worried look in his eyes. "What's up?" she asked.

"I just don't know if I did the right thing," Max said.

"Ditching Ray?" Kylie laughed. "Oh my god, Max ... It's the *best* thing you could have done! Look how unhappy you've been. He basically railroaded you into being something you're not!"

"I know," he said. But he did not sound convinced. "But like he said – and like Danielle said too – it is a business. I didn't like doing it, but lots of people don't like their jobs. And they don't just quit."

"But you're not quitting," Kylie said. Then she looked at him uncertainly. "Are you?"

Max shook his head.

"You can still think of it as a business. Just aiming for a different market." She squeezed his hand. "This is what I do now, remember? I can help you."

"But Ray did that. He got me a huge market."

"Yes," Kylie said, "but it was very mainstream. Not meaning anything against it. But honestly, you won't be missed on that scene."

Max was silent. Kylie worried that she had been too blunt.

"Max, I *love* the stuff that you and Eric do. There's nothing else like it. I'm sure there are more people like me. In fact, I *know* there are! And once they discover you, they'll be hooked. You just need to reach them."

Max sighed. "Well, how are they ever going to find out about me?"

"For one thing, that last song you and Eric wrote, about the environment?"

"It was about waste," Max said. "How we should think about what we *want* versus what we *need*. Not to waste stuff."

"Well, there you go. So you need to link in to people who share those values. And to other people. People like me who like your sound, *and* who like what you stand for."

94

Max looked puzzled. "And how do I get in touch with people like you?"

"Well, how about my Facebook friends for a start? Let's take our picture – me and my amazing musician friend Max on a mountaintop!" She passed her phone to him. "Here, your arm is longer." She put her arm around his waist and snuggled into his shoulder. Max's smile came naturally.

"I'll post it right now," Kylie said and grabbed the phone back. "And then let's go through all your social media stuff. Like I said, I'm happy to help. You on for dinner?"

Danielle looked at her watch. Nearly lunch time. Her mobile buzzed. It was Brook. "Hey, how'd it go?"

"I got the loan!"

Danielle nearly tossed her phone in the air. "Oh my god, Brook. That's fantastic!"

"Thanks to you, Dani! I owe you a big one."

"You did all the work, Brook. Your company is so successful – growing so quickly. And you're right, the imports one is a no-brainer."

"But Dani, that was all true at my other meetings too. But I thought about what you said, about playing their game."

"What do you mean?"

"Well, the briefcase ... I carried it like you said. But then I also thought I should look more business-like too. So I dressed more like they do ... wore my hair back instead of down. I even introduced myself as Brooklyn!"

Danielle laughed. "No one calls you that!"

"I know. But it's Brooklyn Winston Design now. So no more little Brook. Your idea, Dani."

"And?"

"Dani, it was a completely different meeting. He treated me with respect — listened to me more." She sighed. "And of course those summaries you did for me had a huge impact. All the numbers on two pages. He actually read it all!"

"I'm really happy for you," Danielle chuckled. "Brooklyn!"

"Oh god, stop," Brook laughed. Then she caught her breath. "But Dani, I thought you could try the same thing."

"I don't need a loan."

"No, I mean playing the game. Remember you said that woman made some crack about how you dress?"

Danielle sighed. "Yeah. Marie."

"And remember I was saying that you don't look like an accountant?"

Danielle nodded. "Yeah, I remember."

"Well, what if you did? Like you said, play their game a little. I'm not saying you don't look great, but maybe just tone things down in the office. The fashion. *Look* more like an accountant."

Danielle tilted her head. Brook had a point. She did stand out compared to everyone else in the office. And maybe that *wasn't* actually a good thing.

"Dani?" Brook was asking. "I don't mean it as a..."

"No, it's fine Brook," Danielle said. She caught a flash of movement at her door. "I totally get what you are saying. Hang on."

It was Tony, holding a stack of files. He saw that Danielle was on the phone and started to back off, but Danielle motioned him in.

"Sorry Brook, I've got to go. But let's talk more about that. You guys still on for Saturday?"

"Roger got called away again, but I'll be there. Thanks again, Dani."

Danielle said her goodbye and motioned for Tony to take a seat. "Okay, show me the section you're stuck on..."

Brook scanned the room. The stage was empty, but the tables were filling up. Soft jazz music played on the speakers. "This is a different kind of place."

"Yeah. Max actually likes the mellow stuff better. It's one of Eric's friends playing tonight," Danielle said, stretching her neck to look around. "Is that them over there?"

They slipped between the tables to where Max and Kylie were sitting.

"Hey Kylie," smiled Danielle. "Great to see you! This is my friend Brook."

"Hey Brook," Kylie said, turning to Danielle. "Yeah, it's been a while."

"What are you doing these days?" asked Danielle.

97

"She's in marketing, believe it or not," replied Max. "She's actually helping me with my social media stuff, now that I'm going out on my own."

"Ray didn't do that stuff very well anyway," said Danielle. She turned to Kylie. "So where do you work?"

"I'm working for a really cool marketing company," added Kylie. "Here in town. We focus on finding cost-effective and innovative solutions for entrepreneurs and small businesses."

"She's really good at it too," added Max. "You should talk to her, Brook. I bet she could help you a lot."

"Actually," said Brook, "my budget is super-tight right now, with the new arm of the business opening up. And besides, I already have more clients than I can deal with. I don't really need marketing."

Kylie started to respond, but Danielle interrupted. "Oh god, it's Cedric." He was heading straight for their table. She lowered her head.

But Cedric passed by Danielle and strode up to Max instead.

Max's face spread into a grin. "Hey, man!" He stood and put his arm around Cedric.

"Hey everyone, this is Zed. Amazing trumpet player!" Max turned to Cedric. "You playing tonight?"

Danielle stared at Zed. Yes, it really *was* the same Cedric. But he looked different. His hair was lightly gelled, and his dark curls cascaded over his temples. His black jeans looked good on his slender physique, and he wore a casual wool blazer over a T-shirt. He didn't look like a weasley lawyer at all. He looked good!

Danielle had missed what they were saying. Cedric was giving her an awkward look. He turned back to Max. "Thanks, man, but I'll leave you guys to do your thing. I'm here with some buddies anyway." He pointed towards the front.

After he left, Max leaned forward on the table. "That guy is so cool. Amazing musician. But, believe it or not, he's actually a lawyer!"

"How long have you known him?" Danielle asked cautiously.

"I've known *about* him for ages. He does all of this humanitarian work, directing a charity that does environmental stuff. Getting rid of plastic, saving threatened habitat. I got to know him maybe two years ago. Some of my songs were inspired by that, actually. He runs a foundation."

"The song you played me the other day?" asked Danielle.

Max laughed. "Yup, that one especially. Zed asked if I would work with him on their next campaign – provide some of the music. I didn't think I'd have time with all the touring I was going to do. But now I've said yes."

"Wow," said Brook. "He sounds like an amazing guy."

The room had filled up and the band was setting up on stage. Danielle looked towards the front, in the direction Cedric had gone, but she couldn't pick him out in the crowd.

How do you differentiate yourself?

First of all, you need to go back to the two or three attributes you defined for yourself in *Chapter 3 Define How You Want to be Perceived*. If you have a number of products you offer, you can choose attributes for each product or sub-brand. But make sure they don't clash with the attributes of your overall brand. Don't send mixed messages about who you are or what you stand for.

Here are some examples of ways you can differentiate your business or your products. This is not a complete list. See which of these examples might work for you, but also look out for other ways you can showcase your uniqueness and stand out from the competition.

You want people to be happy to pay a premium price for your products and services because no one else does it how you do. You want to be perceived as different and unique.

Uniqueness

Making yourself unique, unlike anything else out there, is one of the best ways to differentiate yourself. Cirque du Soleil is a great example of uniqueness. The traditional circus has been around for centuries, but there is only one Cirque du Soleil.

Cirque du Soleil came up with several traits that make them completely different from any other circus. They created their own niche. First, they have only human performers – no animals. Second, those performers are some of the best in the world: highly skilled gymnasts and dancers and acrobats, able to achieve feats that appear impossible. Third, their performances always have a story line or theme. As a consequence of these traits, Cirque du Soleil was able to define a whole new audience for their circus: adults, rather than children, paying a premium fee for the show.

Cirque du Soleil's uniqueness is the key to its success. From its roots as a small traveling circus founded in Québec, Cirque du Soleil has grown to a multi-million dollar company, with a permanent show in Las Vegas and numerous traveling shows playing around the world.

What about your business? What are you specifically positioned to do that no one else could do the same, or that no one else is doing? How can you do things differently? How can you innovate on a product or service and do it your own way?

Specialization

Specializing means putting yourself out there on the far right end of the Differentiation Spectrum where you will stick out a mile.

Remember, do you want to be a big fish in a small pond or a small fish in a big pond? You can choose.

When one of our clients, Margie, a nutritionist came to us, she was working with everyone. Margie applied to be part of the Clever Bunch program, one of our marketing programs. We knew that her business could be highly successful if she was willing to make her pond smaller, so she did. She soon became known as the specialist nutritionist for high-performance sportspeople, and the instant she changed her pond, her business and income changed completely!

You might think that you can't control the pond size. But you can, by choosing your market! It is one of the smartest yet hardest things to do for a business owner. It doesn't mean that "the other" guys won't come to you anymore; on the contrary, seeing you as a specialist will make them want to work with you even more.

You may be, for example, a massage therapist who serves the general public. Your potential market (your pond) is huge, but you are just one small fish of many, competing against all of the other massage therapists out there. How about you focus on treating elite athletes, or people with back issues, or stressed-out professionals? Your pool of potential clients becomes smaller, but by specializing and positioning yourself as an expert, you are now **the big fish in that smaller pond**, and you will become more desirable and "talkaboutable."

Adding more value

You can also differentiate by going above and beyond your call of duty and adding massive value for your clients and blowing their minds with amazing customer service.

Let's take a look into the world of super-expensive handbags. Hermès is the only designer with two of the world's top-ten purses (price-wise). They designed both the second most expensive purse ($1.9 million) and the sixth most expensive purse at a much more modest $120,000! (We must mention that the second-ranked purse comes with a diamond sling that can be removed and used as a bracelet or necklace … Oh, and an eight karat diamond centerpiece that can be removed and worn as a brooch. Very useful indeed.)

Okay, joking aside. So Hermès sells million-dollar purses. But now go check out a Hermès store and you'll see that most of their purses are priced between $3,000 and $6,000. No, not cheap, but not a million dollars!

For just $5,000 you can insert yourself into the middle of their product range – and feel like you're now a member of that million-dollar club. That's **perceived** value; the products change how the customer feels.

And then there are examples of **real** added value. One of our clients, Dannie, is a mechanic. He recognized the specific needs of busy "soccer moms." They have kids; they need their cars all day; and they don't have time to drop things off and wait around.

They appreciate a clean and welcoming shop. So Dannie's business picks up his clients' cars from their home and brings them back when they're repaired. Dannie figured out how to meet all of his clients' needs and has added real value to their experience. By doing so, he has not only gained more clients, he is also getting paid more. And he is desirable for the "right market."

Adding value means looking for ways that you can provide more value than your competitors. Everyone likes to feel they are getting more than what they paid for; it's simple human psychology you can't ignore. This may mean added services, the way Dannie did. Or it may mean offering bonuses like a VIP membership where you offer extra servicing, or free no-obligation consultations for new clients, or free bonus reports for regular customers, or an amazing guarantee that makes you sweat a little – more on that later.

By providing extra value, you will be seen as generous. We especially encourage businesses to give value to a prospect even *before* asking for a sale. For example, in exchange for someone entering their email on your website (building your database of potential clients) you offer a free guide or cheat sheet. Look for ways to provide value before asking for a sale.

Providing free information also helps create the perception that you are a leader in your space, that you know your stuff, and that you are generous. (This was covered in our section on positioning yourself as an expert, in *Chapter 4 But What if YOU Are the Product*.)

Ask yourself how you can add more value to your clients. How can you "wow" them? How can you create an even more amazing customer experience?

Associating with something or someone "famous"

You can also benefit from the perception people already have of other things, even places, by associating yourself with them.

Think of some of the perceptions most of us have about various countries and what two or three attributes you would associate with them. Such as:

- Germany: safety, reliability (think cars, such as Mercedes, BMW, VW, Audi)
- Switzerland: quality, punctuality, reliability (think chocolate, watches, the Swiss Army knife)
- Italy: taste, decadence, luxury (think food, wine, fashion)
- Japan: hardworking, reliable, quality (think cameras, electronics)
- Sweden: design, style (think furniture, design)

Associating your product with a country means you can tag along with that perception to your benefit. Your product doesn't even have to come from that country! The American ice cream maker Häagen-Dazs employed this tactic to great effect.

"What?" you exclaim. "Häagen-Dazs is American?"

That's right: Häagen-Dazs was founded in New York in 1961 by a pair of Jews. However, the founders decided to associate their brand with Denmark – partly as a tribute to the Danes, who had sheltered many Jews during World War II, but also simply because Denmark is known for its dairy products and the country had a positive image in the USA. Not only is the product not Danish, even the name isn't Danish! Neither the Häagen nor the Dazs. But the original founders thought Häagen-Dazs sounded Danish and liked it (and they put a map of Denmark on their product labels to be sure that the association was there)!

Perception is important but, as we've said before, it does also have to come from a place of genuineness. Häagen-Dazs does that: They provide a premium ice cream product that is creamier than most of the competition, and they don't use stabilizers. Their product *is* high quality. But creating the perception that they are Danish – something memorable that differentiates Häagen-Dazs from their competitors – definitely helps to make them memorable and differentiates them from their competitors.

There are many other things besides places that you can associate with. For example, Max already has strong feelings about the environment. Kylie's given him some good advice: to build on that association so he reaches the people who share his values (and may also buy his music).

This strategy certainly requires a bit of creative thinking. Ask yourself if you can associate your business or product with something or someone well-known.

Offering a guarantee

A guarantee can work extremely well for a business and make you stand out from the rest. It builds trust, so that people who are considering buying from you feel confident: They will worry less that they are taking a risk. They will trust that they will get what they think they should. An example of an effective guarantee is Fedex, proudly proclaiming that if your package does not arrive on time, they will give you your money back. This inspires confidence in their service. (Although they should probably have a guarantee that your stuff won't be broken either!)

A guarantee also puts your butt on the line and makes you work harder, which is awesome!

Many business owners are reluctant to state a guarantee in their marketing blurb because they fear that people will take advantage of the offer and rip them off. However, working with thousands of business owners, we have found that most businesses will give a purchaser their money back if they are unhappy with the services or product anyway. They already **are** offering a money-back guarantee; they are just not stating it in their marketing pieces.

Most customers will never even try to get their money back anyway, as long as you do a good job, which should always be your goal. Although there may be the odd exception, we've found that the benefits of offering (and advertising) your guarantee outweigh the disadvantages. The occasional customer who does ask for their money back probably would have done so anyway. And honestly? Would you want them as your client if they aren't happy?

Playing hard to get

Another way of differentiating your product is by making it appear more desirable because it is **hard to get.** This can be done through scarcity or unavailability, or by creating a sense of urgency about it. It has to be done with integrity though.

Scarcity or unavailability

Products may receive more attention if they are hard to get. This can happen by accident; for example, when an artist dies and his paintings suddenly become more desirable and therefore more valuable because no more will ever be produced.

But scarcity can also be deliberately manufactured. Artists (still alive!) also deliberately give the perception of scarcity by releasing reproductions of their paintings as limited-edition numbered prints: only so many will ever be produced. There is no reason that they *have* to limit their run of prints, but by doing so, they instill a sense of urgency in their clients (What if they run out?) and are also able to command a higher price.

Tech companies use this strategy too, by deliberately orchestrating a gradual release of their products: supply is limited, and so people work harder to get a piece of the pie right away. Again, we can't highlight enough that you have to use this principle with integrity or it will backfire.

Unavailability is tied to scarcity, but it's not exactly the same thing. Here's a story about how lack of availability raised the demand for a product (and therefore its price) dramatically – even though that was not what was intended.

The game Flappy Birds was released in 2013, and by January 2014 it had become the most downloaded free game in Apple's App Store. Flappy Birds was so popular that its creator actually had it removed from both the App Store and Google Play only a month later – supposedly because he felt guilty that it was so addictive!

But Flappy Birds' abrupt unavailability online had a strange effect. The only way to then get a copy was to buy a phone that already had the game pre-installed. Suddenly, phones with Flappy Birds on them were being offered for sale online for prices going well into many thousands of dollars. Lack of availability made people frantic. They were willing to pay **anything** if they still had a chance to get that game.

The concept of unavailability can be very important to consultants. When a consultant appears to be really busy, they become more in demand. (If he's that busy, he must be good!)

Of course, there are situations where, to do your best work and give the best impression, you need to make yourself more available to your clients. But be careful about how you phrase things: Don't tell them you are free any time, any day. That makes it look like you have no clients and may give the perception that you are not very good! Rather, book them in for a week or a month away, but give them a couple of time options. If their need is urgent and they want you sooner, you can still work to "insert" them into your schedule sooner.

An important note here, though: Please do not lie ever, not in your marketing, not anywhere. Unfortunately, too many people are dishonest and it comes back to bite them in the butt. Keep your marketing ethical at all times.

Urgency

Urgency is another way to get your prospects to take action. You see these types of offers all the time. Some examples include:

- On sale, this week only
- This deal is only available for the next 24 hours
- 25% discount for the first ten people
- Limited enrollment, only 50 seats available

Limited-time or limited-number offers can draw attention to a product or make a service more popular. A sense of urgency not only draws attention to the product, it also helps persuade a potential client to buy, and buy now! We do tend to buy stuff, even stuff we don't need, just because it's on sale. For example, you go to the supermarket and come back with some chocolates you didn't need, but they were on special – today only! And it made you feel you were getting a good deal, or you would miss out!

The same goes for services such as signing up for a course because you are afraid it will fill up and you won't have the option to sign up. It seems urgent – and that feeling **urges** you to purchase. And of course, sometimes you truly do need to act fast not to miss out on a great opportunity!

Again, make sure you are not lying about this urgency. If you say one week only, make it one week only, or people won't take you seriously anymore.

Pricing

For most people (other than the extremely rich for whom money is no object), our decision to buy something comes down to our perception of money versus value. If you perceive the value of a product to be greater than the money it takes to purchase it, you will buy. If you perceive the value of keeping that money as greater, you don't buy.

That being said, how products are priced influences our sense of value or worthiness. Think of Rolex, makers of watches that cost many thousands of dollars. Right away, that gives us the perception that, even if we personally wouldn't spend that much money on a watch, they must be really good.

Just as high prices give a perception of quality and value, low prices can do the opposite. Australian discount clothing store Best & Less had a perception problem: people thought that their products were low quality just because they were inexpensive. But when they marketed those same products in a posh store and tripled their prices, suddenly consumers lined up to buy their products.

This also means you need to think carefully about what you give away for free. We've said above it's important to be generous with your information, and to consider offering free products such as online courses or webinars. However, you also must strike a balance and not give the perception that your work or your products don't have value.

Your pricing structure directly influences who comes in your door. Yet sometimes you may be reluctant to raise prices because you fear that you are not good enough (Remember, the influence of our "internal perception" mentioned in *Chapter 4 But What if YOU Are the Product*?), or that it will turn people away, when in fact doing so may end up drawing you more clients, and a different quality of client. For example, a consultant (or a designer like Brook) who raises her prices while adding more value will be perceived as more premium. As a result, she may become **more** in demand to certain people rather than less. People assume she will do a better job because she is more expensive.

It goes without saying that it's never smart to just raise prices for the sake of it. The value you add for your clientele has to exceed the price they pay for it. Sometimes it takes a little bit of testing and measuring to find the perfect and fairest pricing structure.

In some cases, raising prices is the better strategy, but in others, free samples or trials works. It really depends on your business and what you want to achieve. It's important, though, that you consider more than what your production costs are when you set your prices. You must also think about the perception that your pricing structure gives.

Selling experiences

One aspect of marketing we often find our clients overlook is how their marketing makes people **feel**. Business owners often want to extol the benefits of their product – how efficient it is or how tasty it is – but they forget about the emotional involvement their buyers, or potential buyers, may have with it. People often don't remember much about someone or something, but they always remember how it made them **feel**.

Part of selling an experience means selling the "why" instead of selling the "what." Starbucks doesn't just sell coffee; they grant you membership to a special community. Harley Davidson doesn't just sell motorcycles; they sell freedom and they are really great at doing this. A gym doesn't sell you time to slog away on a treadmill; they sell you health, confidence, or sex appeal.

Businesses that focus on selling the "what" often produce marketing pieces that are a bit boring and unappealing. But businesses that talk about the "why," the dreams people have, focusing on the things they **want** rather than the things they **need**, catch our interest. Look at how Harley sells, with their slogan "Live to Ride, Ride to Live". Now that's an experience: Let's get outta here.

Another company that has done a great job of marketing its product focusing on making people **feel** is GoPro. Their product is a wearable sports camera. But have you seen many GoPro ads that go through the camera specs or talk about the quality of the components? Even though the camera is the product, it is not the camera itself that GoPro is selling. It's the **experience** and the feeling you get from that experience. Featuring usually extreme adventures and experiences such as base-jumping, surfing, heli-skiing, and scuba diving certainly get your heart pumping! And their ads are shareable.

GoPro shows fun, action, and adventure. It's cool. It's exciting. You're right there with that person. In fact, you want to *be* that person: adventurous, daring, free. That's what makes you want to get a GoPro. GoPro differentiates by not being just a camera: It's excitement – a way of life. And they are using user-generated imagery to show the realness of it all.

The purpose of marketing and branding is to make people feel something! Someone smart once said, "Whatever you do, make people feel!"

Positioning to be noticed

You want people to notice you, to be aware that you are out there, and that you are the obvious choice for them.

You need to pro-actively position your product to be seen. One company may have a product that is no better than its competition, but they become more popular because they have positioned it as this amazing thing – through visuals, marketing, and press coverage. Larger companies sometimes tend to have a little bit of an advantage because they have the budget for big marketing campaigns. But the good news is that smaller businesses with less money can get amazing results by applying the same positioning and perception principles. Thanks to social media and technological advances, it's never been easier to get noticed for all the right reasons.

> **The more you are differentiated, the more likely you are to be seen and "talked about."**

Sporting goods companies such as surfboard manufacturers are a great example of generating interest and attracting die-hard fans. Every year or two, some clever manufacturers come up with new models to create buzz and excitement. Often, the "new" designs are nearly the same as the old ones, but with slight changes in board shape, or maybe a few new colors. But they create a new model name to create the perception that this is the latest and greatest thing on the market – the new board that everyone wants – and their "new model" will generate attention. It also keeps their fans from going elsewhere.

A large part of standing out, and positioning your products, comes as a result of a well thought-out marketing approach. But unfortunately many people have misconceptions about marketing, or believe that marketing doesn't work for their particular business. Let's clear that up once and for all so you can have an even bigger impact with your business! We'll share what marketing really entails, and why every business needs some form of marketing in *Chapter 8 A Few Words About Marketing*.

Amplifying Perception

Brook pulled out of the drive-through and placed her coffee in the holder on the console. She'd been on the phone all day and was tired of talking, but this was her only opportunity to call Danielle.

Danielle's voice sounded over the speaker. "Hey Brook, what's up?"

Brook replied, "I'm going to have to cancel on our run for tomorrow morning. Sorry."

"Is everything all right?"

"I'm fine; I just had a super-long day. I committed to, like thirty thousand dollars of materials from Indonesia, so it's kind of scary. I just need to have some downtime with Roger tonight and to get a good sleep."

"Sure, no probs," said Danielle. "Umm, do you have a minute to talk right now?"

"Perfect timing; I'm driving home. What's up?"

There was a silence before she spoke. "Well ... remember Cedric?"

Brook racked her brains. She couldn't remember any Cedric.

"Max's friend," Danielle continued. "From the show last weekend?"

"That guy Zed?" Brook exclaimed. "Yes, I *definitely* remember him!"

"Well, I actually know him a bit. From work," said Danielle.

"Really?" asked Brook. "You guys didn't let on."

"Well, it was a bit awkward. He asked me out last week. And I never answered."

Brook paused before answering. "I thought he seemed pretty cool. You didn't like him?"

"Well, I didn't, at first. But I think maybe I actually do," said Danielle. "And I have a meeting with him tomorrow."

"Can you make some excuse about why you didn't answer?" asked Brook. "Maybe hint about doing something this weekend?"

"You think I should?"

"Dani! Yes, I think you should." Brook stopped at an intersection and sipped her coffee. "He seemed like a really cool guy. And Max obviously thinks so."

Danielle was silent.

Brook continued. "Well, think about it. Oh, and while I have you on the line ... I've been meaning to ask you something. That help you gave me with my account summaries was *so* useful. Why don't you do a presentation on that for our

118

Chamber of Commerce members? We have so many small business owners who would love to learn that stuff."

"Brook, I'm terrified of public speaking!" protested Danielle.

"You are an *amazing* speaker!" Brook laughed. "Roger always talks about your speech at our wedding. And next month's speaker just cancelled. Can I slot you in?"

"Oh god, Brook," said Danielle. She sighed.

"Done! Thanks Dani," said Brook. "You'll see. People will love it. I'll put it in this week's mail-out. And good luck with Zed tomorrow!"

Max was not happy. He slid over so Kylie could share the chair with him and pointed at the screen. "And look at this one. *Dude u r past your prime. Stop the wimpy stuff. I liked u when u played real music.*"

"Max," Kylie said. She squeezed into the chair beside him and put her arm around him. "Why are you focusing on the bad comments? You have, like, three bad comments and three thousand good ones."

"But everyone can read them," he said. "And it makes me wonder. Maybe Ray was right. I was packing the houses when I was doing that harder stuff."

"And were you happy?" Kylie asked.

Max stared at the screen. She took his chin in her hand and turned his face to hers. She asked again. "Were you happy?"

Max lowered his eyes. He shook his head.

"You and Eric love playing together," she said. "And you're good. This new sound – what did you call it?"

"Indie-electronica," replied Max.

"It's great. Your writing, and your voice, plus Eric does what he does on the keyboard."

"We wrote that," Max said. "The sound, I mean. We wrote the songs together with that particular sound on the keyboard."

"That's what I mean! What a great combination! It's new, it's different, and I think it's going to catch on." Kylie put her other arm around Max and squeezed him. "It's *already* catching on! What did you call it, again?"

"Indie-electronica," Max replied.

"Okay, you've got to get that word out there more. Is it your own word?"

Max nodded.

"Perfect!" Kylie said with a grin. "So that word is you."

"And Eric," Max added. He smiled half-heartedly.

Kylie squeezed him again. "You just need to have as much confidence in yourself as I do. As those six thousand people liking your Facebook page do!"

Danielle's phone buzzed and the receptionist's voice announced, "I have a Cedric Morrow here to see you."

"Thanks," she said. "I'll be right there."

Danielle stood up and gathered the stack of binders with the Hamilton files. She took two deep breaths then stepped out to the hallway with as much confidence as she could muster. Cedric stood at reception, once again dressed in his plain lawyer's suit and with his hair slicked off to the side. But he had somehow shed that weasley look that Danielle remembered. She thought of how his curls fell across his brow on Saturday night, and those black jeans.

She shook Cedric's hand. "I've booked the conference room," she said and led him down the corridor.

She motioned for Cedric to sit beside her as she slid the top binder from the stack and opened it. But, instead of looking at the files, Cedric touched her elbow lightly and spoke. "Before we start, I just want to apologize."

Danielle looked up in surprise. "For what?"

"Well, first, I had no idea that you're Max's sister. Not that that makes any difference." He shook his head and looked away. "For suggesting we go out last week. That was terribly unprofessional of me. I hope we can just forget it and move forward."

"No," Danielle said, "I'm the one who should apologize. I'm sorry I didn't get back to you. I just..."

Cedric turned back to her and they held one another's gaze for a moment. Danielle smiled and continued. "I just... well, maybe we could do something this weekend?"

Cedric smiled back. "I'd like that."

Danielle flipped a page in the binder. "Let's do what we're supposed to do here. But why don't we catch up on Saturday?"

Cedric led Max and Kylie down a narrow hallway. "Our office space is still small," he said. "But we're trying to direct as much of our funds as possible to go straight towards the goals of *Habitanto*: making this planet a better place for all species – humans *and* everything else. So the small space helps minimize overheads."

They passed a workroom where a young woman poured over a map spread over a large table. "We have two full-time paid employees. The rest are volunteers," said Cedric. "Do you want a coffee? There's something I'd like to talk to you guys about. An idea."

Cedric cleared space at his desk for them to set down their coffees. "Max," he said, "I've been thinking about something. I would like you to write and produce the soundtrack for our next film."

Max choked on his coffee. "What?" he sputtered, looking at Kylie and then back at Cedric.

"They're short films, each one around thirty minutes. This will be our third. The first two have had over four million views on YouTube." He looked at Max. "They *do* make a difference."

"Why me?" asked Max.

Kylie laughed. "Max, you're a great musician."

"That," Cedric agreed, nodding his head, "but also, you're already on message. Your last song was about the oceans. This film is going to be focusing on plastics on the shoreline – visuals of all the junk washed up juxtaposed with pristine areas, wilderness. We've got a great cinematographer on board, but we need a soundtrack. Will you consider it?"

As they drove back to Max's place, Max turned to Kylie. "I'm not sure about this. It feels like I've just committed to do this huge project for free," he ended.

Kylie was at the wheel. "I think it's great," she said. "It's an opportunity, Max. Sure, it's free, as in you don't get money for it. But look what you *do* get. It will put you in front of this great audience ... What did Zed say? ... Millions of views? *And* they are totally the kind of people you want to reach."

"I guess," said Max.

"And besides, producing is what you want to do more of anyway," Kylie continued. "At least that's what you told me."

"That's true," said Max.

"Are people still sending you demo tapes?"

"Two more this week," said Max. "And I didn't even check today's mail yet."

"Are they any good?" asked Kylie.

"A few are," he answered. "Yeah, I would work with some of them."

They were stopped at a light. Kylie turned to him. "So?" she asked. "You going to answer them?"

"Are you my manager now?" Max laughed. "Yes, okay, I will answer them."

Sam seated himself in front of Brook's desk.

"You wanted to talk about something, Sam?" she asked.

"I was just wondering what we're going to do next?" he asked.

Brook looked at him quizzically. "Next? The Indonesian products are going great. And we're as busy as heck!"

"I know, and we've had some great press. But it's still really only one line." Brook didn't look convinced, so he continued. "People are only going to buy so much and then it's done. Or they might just get tired of it."

"Sam, we're already expanding from the textiles to the furniture," Brook said. She leveled her gaze at him. "As you suggested."

"I know," Sam said. "I appreciate that you listen to my ideas. But I've got more. I think we've got to keep expanding. Coming up with new stuff. Or we'll just end up like some kind of one-hit wonder."

Brook sighed. "Sam, I don't really know where you're coming from. The Indonesian line is totally successful. And we *are* already expanding." She shook her head. "It's not like I have unlimited funds."

Brook's phone buzzed. It was Joanna. She pressed the speaker. "I have an Akito Asumi on the line."

Brook and Sam stared at one another. Sam mouthed the words: *The architect?* Brook nodded back in wide-eyed wonder.

"Brook?" came Joanna's voice again. "I have Mr. Akito Asumi on the line for you. Shall I have him call back?"

"No," Brook gulped. "Please put him through."

Amplifying your image means thinking about those two or three attributes you have decided to focus on – and then turning them up. Figure out where you are adding value and which of your attributes are attracting the right people to you. Then work on amplifying them.

You do this by identifying all the touch points you have in your business. Touch points are every single way your clients or prospects are in contact with you; for example, phone calls, shop visits, website, follow-up cards, emails, invoices, business cards. Then take the attributes you've identified of how you want to be perceived and amplify them throughout each touch point. For example, if you want to be perceived as fun, you might make your email signature funny, or put a fun fact onto your invoices, or send out postcards that are funny rather than stiff and boring.

This is a really fun exercise to do, but it requires a bit of lateral thinking! You could even involve your team in this brainstorming activity.

Building on what you've got

Remember, Dannie the mechanic? He is **very** funny. However, when we first met him, Dannie's business was only just surviving and he wasn't amplifying his charisma and fun-ness.

Dannie went to work each day wondering whether he would have enough customers to stay in business. He was searching for a way to expand his clientele. We challenged Dannie to look at what attributes he already had that would distinguish him from all the other mechanics out there and would get him noticed, giving him a loyal following who would keep coming back?

Well, the first things that struck us about Dannie – making him different from any other mechanic in his area – is that he is quirky, super honest and has a great sense of humor. So why not amplify those unique attributes: fun and honesty?

So now Dannie uses his sense of fun and quirkiness and his realness to make himself stand out. He sends each of his customers a thank you card with his oily thumbprint stamped on and drawn into an animal. He's got a whole menagerie of animals that he can draw, so you get something different from him every time you take your car in. Who could forget that? You almost just want your car to have a problem so you get another fingerprint animal in the mail!

Dannie even adds an element of fun to his invoicing. Instead of threats about what will happen if you don't pay up within thirty days, Dannie adds an extra line saying "Hugs from a happy mechanic. Free."

People smile. And they remember.

Dannie's "fun" strategy worked great for him. He no longer stresses about whether the work will be there. In fact, a year and half after implementing these strategies, Dannie's business has expanded to the point that he has three full-time employees working for him, and he has outgrown his space.

Look for all areas where you can amplify your perception. Your marketing pieces, such as paid advertising and social media campaigns, are important. But, as Dannie's example shows, amplification doesn't only come via costly advertising, especially for small businesses. Many aspects of your behavior, your look, your employees' manner of communicating, and your use of social media can also be used to amplify your perception.

Monitoring how you are perceived

Perception is never static. You must work hard at **defining** the perception you want to create, and then at implementing the steps we've outlined above to **build** that perception.

But the work doesn't stop there. You must be vigilant and **monitor** that perception. Figure out which parts of it are relevant and effective and which are not working. Then reassess or reinvent if parts are not working, and amplify the parts that are.

Make sure to involve your team in this process and maintain clear communication with them. Sometimes when team members (or entrepreneurs themselves) get busy, their focus can become less clear. Your whole team must understand exactly how you want your business to be perceived and have clarity about the brand personality they should be portraying when representing the business.

Monitoring your perception includes making sure that you stay on message and are being perceived the way you want. Remember, your perception exists only in other people's heads. And perception can change quickly. You have the power to reinvent that perception if necessary.

If you find that your perception is not what you want it to be, you need to figure out why. Your perception may not be working because you have misjudged your market and need to reassess. Or perhaps your perception was working for a while, but then the market changed around you, trends changed or a new competitor emerged. Monitoring your perception means constantly assessing and reassessing, and then re-imagining or reinventing if necessary.

The British fashion label Burberry was established in 1856. Burberry invented the trench coat, and they became best known for their distinctive plaid patterns, often used in the linings of their garments. They associated themselves with explorers and adventurers including Roald Amundsen and Ernest Shackleton, and were the sponsors of the adventure that came to be the fastest flight between London and Cape Town in 1937. Burberry became an expensive and coveted luxury brand, and they maintained that perception for over a century.

That all changed in the 1970s. The brand started to become popular with British casual culture. Cheap imitation garments mimicking Burberry's designs were produced and sold to the masses, and football hooligans started wearing copies of Burberry's distinctive tartan pattern. Over the years, Burberry's perception went from one of exclusiveness and gentlemanly luxury to common and mass-produced, associated with hooliganism and loutish behavior. The high end clientele Burberry previously had been associated with now wanted nothing to do with the brand.

Perception of your brand or your product may change over time; in fact, it almost certainly will. By actively policing your perception, you will be aware of any adjustments you might need to make, in plenty of time to deal with them, before it's too late. Fortunately, Burberry's management team was paying attention.

Adjusting and reinventing if necessary

In Burberry's case, the company recognized they were in trouble. Their brand's perception had been sliding, and they were no longer able to attract the high-end market they had previously counted on. They knew they had to turn their image around if the company was to survive. They needed to get away from that image of hooliganism and mass-production and recreate the perception of quality, luxury, and exclusiveness.

Burberry employed a number of well thought-out tactics to bring their image back on track. They used celebrity endorsements, choosing very thoughtfully which celebrities would help to associate them with the attributes they wanted to be known for, such as model Kate Moss and actress/activist Emma Watson.

In recent years, Burberry has become very active in using social media to deliberately manage their perception. In fact, they became innovators in marketing by being the first brand ever to reveal its designs on social media through a #tweetwalk online fashion show via Twitter. Burberry also took to charitable outreach projects to cement its reputation as a responsible and caring part of the community. In 2008, they established the Burberry Foundation, which supports charities that help children achieve their artistic dreams, and they later launched a program to support emerging musicians.

Burberry was able to reinvent and turn their image around, and today they are once again known as a high-end, well-respected luxury fashion house. By monitoring their perception, and recognizing early enough that they had a problem, they were able to bring their image back on track.

Perception is fragile

Unfortunately, it's a lot easier and faster for perception to get damaged than it is to build it up in the first place. Perception is fragile – especially now, in the age of online shaming. One poorly thought-out move can damage your brand very quickly.

Think of the reputations that have been shattered by one single episode. The fashion brand Dolce & Gabbana ran into trouble when the two founders (who are gay) announced that they are against adoptions by gay couples and that they disagree with in vitro fertilization. Numerous celebrities, including Elton John and Madonna, criticized them. Courtney Love threatened to burn all of her Dolce & Gabbana clothing. The hashtag #BoycottDolceGabbana garnered 30,000 tweets in less than a week.

The lesson to be learned is that perception is fragile. You can be at the top of the world, but then you express a discriminating opinion or have a dark secret revealed and you go down. Look at Lance Armstrong, once considered the world's most accomplished, and definitely most famous, cyclist. What's he doing now?

If public perception is important to you, whether personally or in business, be careful. You may hold any opinions you want. But remember, in some cases it may hurt you to share them. Be cautious in your actions and dealings and who you associate with: the better known you become, the bigger the story if you fall. Know when it's time to remove yourself from a situation; cancel that interview if you know you are not in the head-space to do it well, and leave that party before people (or you!) drink too much. Leaving at the top is more fun!

A Few Words About Marketing...

Brook rushed in through the front doors.

"Hey Brook," called Joanna. "Brook!"

Brook stopped and peeled off her jacket as she checked her watch. "What is it? I've got a super-busy day."

"I need you to look at this, the newspaper ads. If you want to renew for a second three months, the deadline is tomorrow." She held out a sheet of paper.

"Joanna, sorry. Can you just review it and make a decision? I've got two calls to Indonesia booked for this morning."

Joanna looked at Brook helplessly. "I don't feel comfortable making decisions like that, spending your money."

"Just renew them then," Brook said as she hung up her jacket and strode away down the corridor. She called back, "Oh, please get Sam to come in and see me."

Brook was already busy reviewing her Indonesia files when Sam tapped at her door. "Hey Sam, come in. I'm just figuring out how much to order. Our profit margin's way higher if I go for higher quantities. But it's scary, committing to spend that much." She looked up and gestured for him to take a seat. "Anyway, how are the cushion designs going?"

"Sorry, Brook," Sam replied as he pulled a chair up. "I haven't been able to work on the Savvy Mundo stuff at all. I've been taking the lead in the Brooklyn Winston Designs, like you said. But I feel like I'm just wasting my time on these prospects. I put all this time into visiting their place, talking to them about their ideas, and preparing them a quote. And then they keep saying they can't afford it."

"But our clients have always been the other way around. Almost like money is no option to them," said Brook.

"I know, and we still have some like that. The Faluccis are great. But I've been getting a lot of calls out of the blue. I think I'm doing everything right. They like it. But then it always ends up that they say it's not in their budget."

"The Faluccis heard about us from the Smythes. So did the Muellers. But you say these people are just calling up out of the blue? How are they hearing about us?"

Sam shook his head. "I have no idea. But the last month or two, there've been way more of these calls that go nowhere."

"Well, maybe we can train Ming up to have her field some of those calls. I need you on the design. I'm confirming the first shipment of fabrics today." Brook said. She looked at her watch. "In fact, they'll be calling any minute. I need your designs ready to go before those fabrics arrive."

Max opened the box. "Pepperoni or mushroom?"

Kylie was seated on the floor with the laptop open in front of her. "How about one of each? And a napkin."

She scrolled through the windows as she chewed. "Look, you haven't posted to Facebook or Instagram for over a month! How are your fans going to remember you even exist?" She exclaimed. "And you're not on Twitter?"

"I don't really have anything to post," said Max. "Especially now, with no new shows booked."

Kylie leaned back and rolled her eyes. "Max. Remember, it's social media. *Social!*"

Max looked at her quizzically.

"People are not going to follow you or friend you if all you do is advertise when you have a show. They want to feel like they *know* you." She looked at him earnestly. "Give them behind-the-scenes stuff. Hint that you're working on a new song. Post pictures so people think they're getting a private peek, like you in the studio. Or on top of a mountain getting inspired!"

"Yeah, I could do that," said Max. He passed her the pizza box. "Ready for another?"

"Sure," she said, and grabbed a slice. "Don't broadcast — *engage* with people. *Social* media, remember? If you wait until you have a show booked, they'll feel like you're just marketing to them. But if you engage with them, they'll perceive you as a friend. And they'll be hanging out for you to announce a new show!"

Danielle was already seated at a table by the window when Brook arrived.

"Hey stranger," she grinned, as Brook sat down. "I got us a bottle of Cabernet; hope that's okay?"

"Perfect," Brook smiled as Danielle filled her glass. "Sorry, this last month has been crazy!"

"Cheers," said Danielle. "Crazy good, I hope?"

"Totally," said Brook, and they clinked glasses. "Those fabrics came in, and they are even nicer than I'd expected. Sam's designs are fantastic — I'm so lucky to have him — and we're already in production. Cushions, table runners, bedspreads, you name it."

"That's great, Brook. No wonder I haven't heard from you."

"Sam found an artisan woodworker, so we're going to create our own custom line of upholstered furniture too," Brook continued. "And Kylie is amazing."

"I know," said Danielle. "Max is so much happier now."

"I mean she's amazing for me," replied Brook. "I'm happy for Max too. But he convinced me to get Kylie to help with my marketing. I was kind of reluctant, but he's right. She's saved me so much time. Now I can do what I'm supposed to do and not run around doing everything kind of half-assed."

"Like what?"

"Streamlining things. Thinking about who I'm aiming for," said Brook. "Now we can direct our marketing towards the clientele we want and adjust how they perceive us."

"Did that magazine feature help?" asked Danielle.

"Totally! It got us some good high-end clients. But it also brought in a lot of people who saw us there, then found us in the newspaper or online, but who basically can't afford us." She chuckled. "Or, as Kylie puts it, who *we* can't afford to deal with!"

Danielle passed a menu across to Brook. "Hey, I guess we should look at the food while we're here! Anyway, I'm glad that's working out for you."

Brook opened the menu. "And she's training Joanna up to do our social media stuff. And rejigging the website too."

"Wow, sounds like a lot of work," said Danielle.

"Like I said, I was kind of reluctant at first. But she's even created these automated tracking systems. They keep *way* better records *and* save me time. So it's less work and it makes it really easy for me to oversee everything!" She glanced briefly down at her menu. "Anyway, how are things with you?"

Danielle leaned in and smiled. "Really good."

Brook laughed. "You're seeing that guy? Zed?"

Danielle cocked her head and looked down. "Kind of. We've gone out a few times. I guess, yes."

"Hey, that's great news. Congrats!" Brook raised her glass. "And Max? Sounds like he and Kylie are back together?"

"Yup," Danielle said as they clinked their glasses. "They've been hanging out for a few weeks. But now it's 'official.' I haven't seen him this happy for years."

What is marketing, anyway?

Marketing encompasses all the strategies you use to attract people to your business; it is the oxygen that feeds your business. Influencing the perception others have of you is part of your marketing. Many business owners have had bad experiences with marketing and as a result believe that marketing doesn't work for them. However, it is often not the marketing channel to blame but how the channel or strategy is being used. And perception plays a big role.

Many marketing campaigns fail because business owners do not have clarity on their positioning. It's not a failure of the marketing pieces themselves. It's that their message has not been thought through. You need to define the perception you are aiming for first, before you launch into marketing campaigns, so that everything ties together and you present a consistent image. All your marketing pieces have to pull in the same direction.

Think about this: What is your perception of a diamond? What does a diamond symbolize to you? Perhaps love? Or maybe style, wealth, or power?

Believe it or not, until little over a century ago, diamonds were not highly valued as gemstones. Unlike the more brilliantly colored gemstones such as rubies, emeralds, and sapphires, the colorless diamond looked pretty plain. The high prices that diamonds commanded were only because they seemed scarce.

That changed in the late 1800s when huge diamond deposits were discovered in South Africa. De Beers Consolidated Mines managed to take control of these deposits. But the high price on diamonds had been based only upon their scarcity. Now that there was a sudden abundance of diamonds, it was important for De Beers to maintain the *perception* of scarcity, so they could justify high prices for their product. So they built a monopoly to control supply. Cecil Rhodes, the founder of De Beers, knew that the only challenge to his company's success would be if any more diamond deposits were discovered, threatening his monopoly.

That happened in 1898. The new mine's owner, Ernest Oppenheimer, refused to join the De Beers cartel. However, Oppenheimer realized that, to maintain the perception that diamonds are scarce in order to keep prices high, he had to limit production.

By 1929, the De Beers mines had been taken over by the Oppenheimer family who, by then, had also managed to get control of more recently discovered deposits in other countries. So the Oppenheimers were still able to preserve their monopoly on production and supply. But now, with so many diamonds available, maintaining the illusion of scarcity by stockpiling their product no longer made financial sense. They needed to somehow raise the demand, and the price, for their diamonds.

So they launched a sophisticated advertising campaign, led by a New York agency. They eventually came up with the idea of linking diamonds with romance and love.

This was the period when motion pictures were just becoming big. Diamond promoters managed to get the gems written into film scripts. Glamorous stars such as Katherine Hepburn, Bette Davis, and Ginger Rogers showed off their glittering diamonds, both on- and off-screen.

The perception became that diamonds symbolize love and commitment. A new cultural tradition – the engagement ring – was born. You're probably already familiar with what has become one of the most famous advertising slogans of all time: "A diamond is forever."

Through careful management of perception, first De Beers and then later the Oppenheimers completely transformed both the price and the demand for diamonds. The diamond was once considered to be a plain, semi-precious stone, but the illusion of scarcity caused it to be perceived as special and more valuable. Then, with their diamond stockpiles growing, producers were able to increase demand for the stones by convincing an entire culture that a diamond is **the** symbol of true love.

All of that was achieved through changing perception.

Common misconceptions about marketing

We have found that there are some common misconceptions about marketing that are holding business owners back from achieving great results. A lot of business owners struggle with how to go about marketing, why **every** business needs it, and how to tailor a marketing campaign exactly to your own company's needs (there is no one-size-fits-all solution). Look at all the excuses Brook had for why she didn't need marketing. Yet her employees were wasting time with enquiries that did not lead to sales, and she didn't even know, at first, where those leads were coming from!

Unfortunately, many business owners make up a lot of excuses to not market, based on misconceptions. And it's to their detriment. So let's go through some of the most common misconceptions that people have about marketing.

No need to understand marketing

Most people go into business because they are good at something, or they are passionate about something, or they see an opportunity. Maybe they love sailing and want to turn their passion into a way of life by starting a sailing school. Or they've been working as a hairdresser for five years and like the job, but they think they would earn more by going out on their own. Or they see a niche in the publishing field that no one is filling and think they could succeed at.

These are all great reasons to start a business. **But being good at what your business does doesn't necessarily mean that your business will succeed.** (If only it were that easy!) Once you go out on your own, in addition to being good at whatever you offer, you also need to learn some business skills – and marketing is a huge part of running a business. Even the most skillful person at their craft can completely fail in business if nobody knows about them.

Look at some of the world's most successful entrepreneurs. If you think about someone like Richard Branson, what is he really good at? Do you think he built Virgin Records because he was the world's best sound technician? (Umm no). That guy is amazing at marketing and getting publicity.

Same for the founder of Apple Computers. Whenever Apple was launching a new product or campaign, Steve Jobs would spend an hour nearly every day with his marketing team. There have been other super smart technical people with ideas that would rival those of Apple, but if nobody knows about them, they don't stick around very long. Marketing gets the word out.

If you plan to be in business now and in the future (which we're sure you do, otherwise you wouldn't be reading this book), it's smart to perceive yourself as a lifetime student of marketing. Yep, that's right! Keep reading and keep learning for life.

Not ready for marketing

If you don't have enough clients, you need marketing. If you *do* have enough clients at the moment, and plan on still being in business in the future, you also need marketing. Even if you haven't even launched your business yet, you already need marketing! You can't just hang up your business sign and think that customers will automatically line up.

> **There is no such thing as not being ready for marketing. Every business, of any size or at any stage, needs marketing.**

Your start at marketing does not have to be big or expensive. Depending upon your industry, and how mature your business is, your marketing may be little more than a website landing page and an active Facebook account. Larger companies, or those seeking expansion, might require more extensive marketing campaigns. (Our first book, *Bananas about Marketing*, goes through all of this).

No time for marketing

Marketing is the life-blood of your business. Yes, it takes time now and you don't always see the results right away, but saying that you don't have time for marketing is like saying you don't have time to eat. Sure, you could survive for a few weeks, maybe even a month or two. But you are not going to survive in the long term.

Marketing is the same way. It may not seem like it has value today, but it is an investment in the future of your business.

The longer you are in business, the more you will realize that your to-do list never goes away. It's something that you live with, and there will always be more tasks to do than you can humanly get done. However, if you are only working **reactively** (in other words, problem-solving), and never **proactively** (investing in your business's future), you will keep yourself busy and feel like you are being productive ... until one day you find yourself wondering, "What happened? How did my business end up in such a bad state?"

When undertaking a new marketing campaign or investing in a new type of marketing, you don't always know what your results will be. That uncertainty definitely leads to procrastination for some. You simply must force yourself to make time to do new things, which will force new results to happen. Invest your time now, and you will reap the benefits in the future.

No money for marketing

If you really can't afford marketing, this basically proves that you can't afford *not* to market. If your finances are that tight, you definitely need to drum up some more business!

In most cases, when starting a business, people have more time but limited money (unless they have investors). As the business grows, there is generally more money available to invest back into the business but, as the business owner gets busier, there is less time.

For a business to grow, you have to invest either time or money. It is smartest at the beginning, when finances are tighter, to use marketing strategies that don't cost the world (rather than going into crazy debt). However, as soon as there are funds available, it is definitely worth investing some of those earnings into paid strategies that will accelerate growth. (Yup, you might have to skip that trip to Bali or the Caribbean ... just for a while ... but your business will thank you!)

One question we are often asked is: "How much should I budget for my marketing?" It's definitely hard to give a definite answer to that, and of course the importance of marketing depends on your business. But you do need to outlay something to generate results and so that you can start to figure out what works for you. You need to be proactive.

The key is to track whether you are getting a return on your investment or not. So, for example, if you are spending a thousand dollars per month on a marketing strategy that is bringing in an extra $3,000 (after expenses), you are winning. If you've found a formula, look for ways to scale it up. If your formula isn't producing results, then investigate alternatives.

A common mistake we see is that, when times get tough for a business owner, they tighten things up by turning off their marketing. The default reaction is: "Where can I stop spending to make up the money to cover this bill?" This is a great question to ask when things are tight, to make sure you are not spending unnecessarily. But remember, money spent on marketing is what's going to generate sales. It may seem tough to continue with those costs when the payoff is not instantaneous, but the alternative is losing your future income – and possibly your business.

Another approach is to ask "How can I generate more sales to cover this bill?" This approach not only keeps your mind open to new possibilities, it pushes you to play at a higher level and find new opportunities. Once the bill is paid, often you will then be generating more income because of your investment, which then helps you to avoid falling into this situation again in the future.

No need for marketing as I have enough clients!

We could pretty much summarize this whole section with a single word: Apple.

Apple has more than enough clients. But they've always understood that marketing is less about today than it is about tomorrow.

Even if you believe you have enough clients right now, if you focus too much on your current contracts or current production or current sales, you are not ensuring that you will still have enough clients (or any at all) next year, or in five years.

We often see entrepreneurs who immerse themselves in producing good work with a client. But then, when the contract finishes, they are left scratching their heads, wondering where their next client will come from. At this point they think they had better start marketing.

But marketing is not just a one-time activity, with the goal of quickly trying to hunt down a client. Marketing is an ongoing process. Doing it right will help you avoid the ups and downs in business. If you have done your marketing well, by the time you are nearing the end of that contract, you will have the next one already booked ... plus a few leads of people who have expressed interest in your services. Then there will be a dozen others you haven't even had contact with yet, but who have heard of you and just might end up giving you a call in six months or a year.

There is a Chinese proverb that summarizes this point perfectly: "The best time to plant a tree was twenty years ago. The second best time is now." Don't wait!!

My business is different

Yes, yes, you are special ... Everyone is special.

It's human nature to want to feel a bit special. Sure, we all are different and distinct in our own right, and so are our businesses. When it comes to marketing, however, the same foundational principles apply to every single business.

If you offer something and people are paying you money for it, you need marketing to sell more of it. It doesn't matter whether you are selling a product, widget, an app, your knowledge, a skill, your time, or anything else; the better your marketing is, the more you will sell. And, as you raise your profile, you will be able to charge more for the same transactions.

Even if they are not out to make money, non-profits and charitable organizations also benefit from marketing. They still need to actively market to spread their message and get people to come forward to help raise awareness, or funds, or whatever else it is that they are out to achieve.

One of our former clients, Ryan, a chiropractor, used to believe that traditional marketing didn't work for him. His business was doing okay, but he was looking to expand it by growing his clientele, with the aim of employing one or two more chiropractors further down the track. He had tried many marketing strategies, which hadn't paid off: Google Ads, blogging, local newspaper ads, letterbox drops, networking, and more. He literally came to us saying, "My business is different. Normal marketing doesn't work for me."

We looked over what he had tried, and we pretty much immediately saw ways to improve his results. Ryan had concluded that the **means** of his marketing – ads, blogging, whatever – didn't work for him. But what we saw was that the **image** his materials gave was off the mark and sending mixed messages. We helped him to work on that perception, picking his attributes to focus on and creating a new perception of him as the expert, which includes the words that he used, the imagery, the colors, and so on. Almost immediately, the results of his marketing began to improve.

If you think that your business is different, that marketing just does not work for you, you have probably been doing it the wrong way. Whatever you're selling, you are no different! Better marketing delivers better results.

Trendsetters

"Thank you, everyone, for coming," Brook said. She scanned the faces around the table. It seemed incredible that they were all here because of her; that she had built this company herself!

"As you all know, we've been growing rapidly," Brook continued. "We haven't had a chance to all get together for a while. But I want to update you on some changes that will be happening to both Brooklyn Winston Design and Savvy Mundo."

She looked around the table at her employees' expectant faces. "As most of you know, we've been talking to Akito Asumi."

"Who's that?" asked Janice.

"Only one of the world's most famous architects!" said Sam.

"He's from Japan, but he works all over the world," continued Brook.

"Open concept stuff," added Sam. "Japanese inspired, but not traditional at all."

"Really cool," added Ming.

"Yes, simple but elegant," said Brook. "Well, believe it or not, Akito Asumi wants to work with us."

"He must have seen us in that magazine article," said Ming.

"And he obviously liked what he saw," added Brook, nodding. "He said he's wanted to partner with an interior design team for some time. And he's decided he wants it to be us."

"But what will that mean?" asked Gustavo.

"Well, definitely some changes for you guys on the design team. Sam is going to continue with the lead on the Indonesian line for now, and Gustavo, I want you to work with him. Keep the new ideas coming." Brook turned to Ming. "And Ming, you and I are going to work on the Japanese line. Basically same concept: We select and import fabrics and other textiles from Japan and incorporate them into a new line of furniture and accessories."

"Does this mean you're going to have to get another bank loan?" asked Ming.

"Akito is willing to invest in this. We're still figuring exactly how that's going to work, probably some sort of partnership." Brook turned to Janice. "So our finances will be getting more complicated. But it means that I can finally get Janice on full-time." Janice smiled at the thought of that.

"Wow, this is great news, Brook," said Ming.

"And there's more," continued Brook. "It's going to be busy for the four of us in design. So, over the coming months, I'll be looking to hire two more designers. And Joanna is already doing much more than reception work, so she'll gradually move to becoming our office manager, and eventually I'll hire a new receptionist."

Gustavo looked worried. "Are you sure you can afford all this?" he asked. "I mean, the Indonesian designs are nice. And selling well right now. But they're already being copied. What if sales drop and you can't afford it all?"

Brook turned to Sam. "You want to answer this one?"

Sam smiled. "Have you seen those copies? They're cheap; they're not even sewn well. Sure, they're out there. But the people who want quality won't touch them."

Gustavo said, "I know the quality is crap. But we're already seeing a lot of those knock-offs around. It makes ours look not so exclusive anymore."

"And that's why you and I are going to keep brainstorming," responded Sam, thumping his fist on the table. "Always having something new in the works. Keeping ahead."

Brook's life seemed like a whirlwind. She had wanted success. She had wanted her companies to grow. But she hadn't realized how exhausting success would be. She was glad to get into her car and head toward home.

She flicked on the radio. The announcer was talking about some "hot new duo," but it wasn't until he mentioned the word "indie-electronica" that she realized they were featuring Max and Eric.

She speed-dialed Danielle. "Dani? Turn on your radio!"

"I'm listening to it!" Danielle responded breathlessly. "Kylie called me to say they were going to be on."

"You knew already? How did they score that?"

"You know Kylie!" Danielle laughed. "She's been pushing them to get out there more. She wrote a press release, saying what innovators they are, how they are the founders of the whole indie-electronica scene. She got them to make a short demo tape, and they sent it all out to a bunch of radio and TV stations."

"Wow, good for them!" Brook said. The announcer had finished the interview and was sending Max and Eric up to the mics to play live. "Oh, I want to hear this!"

"Me too. I'll talk to you later," said Danielle. Brook hung up the phone as the haunting sounds of Eric's keyboard and Max's rich voice floated through her car.

Danielle paused at the door to Mr. Frank's office. "You wanted to see me, sir?"

"Ah, Danielle." Mr. Frank stood up, smiled, and gestured to the chair. "Come in, sit down."

Danielle took the seat across from Mr. Frank's desk, and tried not to look worried as he settled back into his chair.

"I hear from Cedric that you and he have been working very well together." Mr. Frank looked up and raised an eyebrow. "Very well."

Oh no, thought Danielle. *Does he know?*

"He says you are very professional," Mr. Frank continued. "Very thorough."

Danielle allowed herself a quiet sigh of relief. "Cedric is very professional too," she said. "And thorough."

"And I'm pleased to see you working more with some of our new employees. Both Tony and Hatsuo speak very highly of you." Mr. Frank picked up a sheet of paper from his desk. "And it reflects in the quality of work they are producing already."

"Thank you, sir," said Danielle.

"But the main reason..." he started, and glanced down at the paper in his hands. "I see you're giving a talk at the Chamber of Commerce."

Danielle nodded. "Yes. I've been helping some friends who own their own businesses. I realized there is a need..."

Mr. Frank interrupted her. "I'm impressed, Danielle. Very impressed."

"Actually, Mr. Frank, I've been thinking..." Danielle said.

Mr. Frank nodded for her to go on.

Danielle took a deep breath. "Our accounting strategies mostly focus on corporates. But there are a lot of entrepreneurs – consultants and small business owners – who need accounting services. Something more geared towards their scale of business."

Danielle hoped she hadn't said too much. But Mr. Frank was gazing at her expectantly, so she continued. "I think there's an empty niche there. I was thinking we could look at opening a new arm to our business, geared towards smaller enterprises."

Mr. Frank leaned back and was silent for a moment. Then he leaned forward. "I like it. That's thinking outside of the box. I like it, Danielle. Why don't we schedule a meeting to discuss this further when Mr. Jones is in too. Say, early next week?"

"You wanted to see me, Sam?" Brook peered into Sam's office.

"Oh, sure," he said, rising quickly. "Hang on, let me get Gustavo."

Sam flew out the door and returned a moment later with Gustavo.

"So," said Brook as she sat down, "it looks like you two are working well together. How are the Japanese designs coming along?"

"We're getting there with them. We'll have some ideas to present to you by the end of the week," Sam said. "But there's something else we wanted to run by you." He turned and looked meaningfully at Gustavo.

"I was wondering about Bolivia," Gustavo said. Brook looked at him quizzically, so he continued. "Doing the same as you did for the Indonesian fabrics, and now the Japanese ones. Doing it with Bolivian materials, combining them with our own unique design."

"Bolivia?" Brook asked. She paused then shook her head. "I don't know the first thing about Bolivia!"

"I was born there," said Gustavo. "I was a baby when we came here, but we always went back every few years."

"Brook," Sam exclaimed, "he has cousins who are weavers! So we could already start with contacts."

Brook gazed at the wall. "Let me think about it." Then she turned back to Gustavo. "Do you think they could send us some samples?"

"I can ask them," Gustavo said.

Being a trendsetter in your field is a great goal to go after! It will not only help you be seen as a leader, it will also make it harder for your competition to copy you as you are always one step ahead. It also keeps your business cutting-edge, avoiding going "stale."

Being a trendsetter means you are innovating, or at least improving on something. You don't have to reinvent the whole wheel. Quite often, a new trend is just a slight variation on something that has been done before, or something that was "out" for long enough that now it is back in. Look at fashion trends that come and go, such as mini-skirts, bellbottoms, dirty denim, or toe socks.

Trends are short-lived

The word "trend" means the general direction something is heading to or changing toward. Trends are not static things.

By the time the bulk of the population has caught on to a trend, it's often already out. If you want to be a trendsetter, you need to be thinking ahead of your market in order to stay current. And you must always keep in mind that your trend will have a limited life span.

What is a trend, anyway?

A trend is, fundamentally, a perception. The sport of windsurfing didn't change dramatically (other than some advances in technology) between its invention in the mid-sixties, its peak in popularity in the eighties, and its rapid decline in the nineties. But people's perception of it sure did, as the trend ran its course.

The same goes for workout programs from aerobics (that's *so* eighties!) to CrossFit. They weren't trends because they once were useful and then suddenly stopped being effective. They became trends then declined in popularity only because people's **perception** of them changed.

How long does a trend last? How does it even start? And why? ... Some good questions!

Let's use those fashion trends that come and go all the time, as an example.

Trends start with those known as the "early adopters." Something gets those early adopters to wear something different. Maybe she saw the abundance of velvet on the catwalk at the last fashion show, or maybe he liked Don Draper's pocket square in Mad Men. But, whatever it is they saw, they liked it, they wanted to look like that too, and they started wearing it themselves.

According to one fashion expert, early adopters account for only a tiny percentage of those who will eventually participate in the trend. However, they are the most influential. We see them walking down the street, or at the restaurant, or the bar on Saturday night. If they are celebrities or people in the spotlight, the trend will take off even faster. We notice them, and we want to stand out like that too.

So in come the imitators. The first wave of imitators helps the trend grow. Then in come the late adopters. Now everyone is wearing it! (Except, of course, the early adopters. They have already moved on to the next great thing!)

And that is the cycle of a trend. How long it lasts depends a lot on what the trend is. In fashion, trends may last for as little as one or two seasons, or up to a few years. Trends in so-called "health foods" seem to last a year or so. They are usually set off by some published study (often funded by the product's manufacturer, unfortunately) that claims food prevents disease, or promotes good health, or helps with weight loss. Next thing you know, everyone is talking about kale, quinoa, ancient grains, or chia seeds. Or about blueberries, acai berries, or goji berries – or whatever next year's miracle berry is going to be.

Trends in sport tend to last longer – a year or even several years. Look how the range of fitness classes offered by gyms has evolved over the years: from aerobics to kick-boxing to spinning to core to CrossFit to HIIT, Tabata and circuit training, to Xtend Barre. Each one has lasted for a few years. What's next?

How to become a trendsetter

You don't need to be a trendsetter to be successful. But it certainly helps! Trendsetters start way over on the far right side of the Differentiation Spectrum: highly differentiated. Then, as they are copied by others, their product becomes less unique and they slowly get pushed over to the left.

The truth is that starting a new trend is not easy. There are no guarantees that your idea or your "thing" is going to catch on. But there definitely are steps you can take to increase the odds.

A fundamental to starting a trend is that you must begin with a great product. (This totally ties in with our earlier advice about being genuine: Your product has to be the "real deal" or it will not catch on for long.) Trends depend so much upon publicity, word-of-mouth, or going viral that if your product is not special, news about it will not get passed on. What you make or do must provide quality or results, or be useful.

Then you've just got to make people – ideally some influential people – want what you have to offer. **You have to make your product irresistible to them.** If you can get *some* people to want it badly enough (those early adopters), they will get one. As more and more people see "it" and want one too, your "thing" starts to catch on and they get one too. And there you go – you've created a trend.

Obviously, this is not so easy to do. (If it were, everyone would be a trendsetter.) There is no surefire way to make your product or your idea into the next new trend. But here are some things you can do to increase your chances.

Targeting the influencers

Remember what we said about getting the trend to start to catch on? This is where you need a few people to start using your product – ideally influential people.

Influential people don't necessarily have to be famous. People who are more confident and daring tend to be the people who will take the risk of trying something new. That means that they are the people who will, by their very nature, become early adopters of things. They also have the type of personality that others look up to, so they are influential too. Simply by having, wearing, or using your product, these people are influencing others: their friends, and family, as well as people who see them on the street. If those others decide to try it, your trend will catch on.

Then there are the **really** influential people, and that's where we get into celebrity endorsements. Big companies sink millions of dollars into celebrities because it works. In fact, many pro athletes earn much more from their advertising contracts than they do playing their sport. Sprinter Usain Bolt reportedly earns over $20 million a year, by far the most ever for a track and field athlete, and nearly all of that comes from his product endorsements ($9 million from sportswear manufacturer Puma alone).

Not only do celebrities appear in these companies' advertising, they often also personally endorse their sponsors' products. For example, Bolt tweeted about how Gatorade "does the trick" for him after a training session. Kim Kardashian reportedly charges up to $1 million to tweet an endorsement about a product.

The fact that the big companies are willing to sink so many millions of dollars into celebrity endorsements of their products shows that the opinions of these influential people are important to us. We look up to them, and we want to be like them. Yup, we are sheep, folks.

So if Usain Bolt flashes a Visa card, we might feel like we're part of his crowd by flashing our own Visa card too. If Kim Kardashian wears Skechers, many of us will probably want Skechers too (or avoid Skechers for the rest of our lives!). If Madonna is drinking coconut water then, hey, maybe we should. And if Oprah or Ellen tells us to read a book – well, that's every author's dream because that book is sure to be topping the best-seller lists the following week.

Being controversial

Stimulating controversy and polarizing, if done right, can be a good way to set a trend. (But beware, they can backfire too. Remember how Dolce & Gabbana's comments against adoptions or in vitro fertilization by gay couples got them into trouble.)

Being controversial means going against what popular thought is at the moment. It is essentially going **against** the norm. It can gain you a lot of attention, and if people catch on and start following you, it can help you to start a new trend.

You can be controversial in many ways. One is simply your look, if you go against the establishment: take the hippies of the sixties, the punk counter-culture that emerged in the seventies, or the goths who appeared in the eighties.

And of course you can be controversial by the things you believe in and voice, but just think very carefully when saying controversial stuff and make sure you truly believe in it and don't just say things to get attention! **In this digital age, everything you say gets recorded forever.** Somebody, somewhere, took a screenshot of that tweet you posted late last night. You can delete it or even deny it, but what you say lives on.

Being controversial works most in your favor if you take the approach of doing things differently – not following the crowd but leading. Being controversial only for the sake of stirring people up (or because you simply did not think before you spoke) will likely backfire on you.

Being controversial can also help with getting publicity. The media needs to talk about different opinions, so they specifically seek out the controversial ones. Controversy sells. And controversy attracts early adopters and loyal followers.

The most important thing, though, is that you mean what you say. Don't just be controversial for the sake of it.

Reinvention

Inventing something completely new and never seen before is not the only way to start a trend. Most people are not inventors, and you absolutely don't have to be one! Re-inventing works as well.

Reinvention can mean bringing something old back to a different generation, so that "old" thing is new to them. Look at the resurgence and popularity of old technologies such as vinyl records, movies shot on real film, and Polaroid cameras. The older generation was captivated when photography turned digital – no more going to the printer! But teenagers today are captivated by a Polaroid camera that actually instantly prints a photo! (Apparently they are also impressed by car windows that you open manually by winding a handle. Cool!).

Reinvention can also mean tweaking something that is existing today. We've mentioned how manufacturers of sporting goods such as surfboards and running shoes are experts at this. Every few years they tweak their design with slight changes to the shape of a board or changing the drop in a running shoe sole – always presenting the package in a new array of the most recent trending colors. Add in a good marketing campaign so this "new" model is seen and suddenly everyone wants that greatest new thing.

This is kind of what Brook is doing. Her first idea, combining Indonesian textiles with western design, was new. But now, doing the same thing with Japanese (and possibly Bolivian) textiles ... well, all she is doing is tweaking that successful recipe.

Naming things

It's all in the name!

We just talked about how sporting goods manufacturers create new models of their products by making only minor changes. Well, they also give each new model a new name. For example, Nike running shoes include the Nike Air, the Lunaracer, the Pegasus, and the Nike Free. Each name evokes an image and appeals to a different type of runner.

Look at the names Ford gives to their cars:

- the compact is a "Pinto" (sounds small and sturdy)
- their full-size is a "Galaxie" (sounds expansive)
- their sports car is a "Mustang" (sounds fast and a bit, well, wild!)

Apple was a master at naming their products so that new models could piggyback on the trend. From the iMac came the iPod then the iPhone and the iPad. Not to mention the various apps or arms of the company: iTunes and the iStore.

This also works for services. For example, different levels of consulting or account packages can carry different names,

Don't go for the boring silver, gold, and platinum, or whatever. Choose names that are more exciting or unique and in line with your brand.

Think of names that reflect what you aim to portray. Brook's new company names totally reflect what she is trying to achieve: "Brooklyn Winston Design" sounds so much more up-market (and expensive) than "Designs by Brook". "Savvy Mundo" gives a different feel, sounding new, innovative, and global. And look how far Max's concept of "indie-electronica" is taking him!

Look at our own company's name. One of our companies, our marketing education organization, is called Basic Bananas, which is a perfect fit for us. First of all, it says who we are: people who love fun (and maybe are a bit "bananas"). Second, it filters through to our target audience. People who are conservative and traditional will probably give us a miss (and they are not who we want to work with anyway). But people who are adventurous and creative and into trying something new will probably give us a second look. And Basic Bananas definitely stands out from the other more staid and traditional marketing firms out there.

Blending products or ideas

Blending things is another great way to trend set and innovate. You take two components (or more) and blend them. These can be very simple things – such as combining two basic products or a product with a service – or they can be quite complex blends of technologies. Max may not realize it, but he is using this technique well. First, with the name for his sound, "indie-electronica." But also in his greater over-arching concept: combining his message for social change and a clean environment with his indie-electronica music.

Here are some other examples that show a range of combinations:

- popchips: combining two food products, popcorn and chips, to create a new product
- online dating: combining two activities – shopping and dating
- the treadmill desk: combining an obligation (work) with a need (health/exercise)
- active meetings: multi-tasking by walking and meeting
- active wear: combining a need (exercise clothing) with a desire (fashion and looking good)
- Xtend Barre: combining two forms of exercise, ballet and Pilates
- the smartphone: combining numerous technologies, including a telephone and a messaging system and a camera along with numerous computing abilities
- drive-through banks: combining a service (banking) with a convenience (not having to get out of your car)

You can innovate and trend set by looking at products or concepts from within your own industry. However, as many of the examples above show, you should look *outside* your own industry too, and think about how you could bring ideas from elsewhere into your own.

Invest!

Okay, so you have that great quality product out there and it's tested and giving good results. People are starting to use it. Maybe you've targeted a few influencers and invited some of the local press to try it out, and the local newspaper has promised to write an article.

So what next?

You have to invest in it! Money (or time) invested can accelerate how fast someone knows about you, your product, or your service.

Many trends catch on because someone, somewhere, planned their marketing campaign. Remember the millions of dollars the big companies like Gatorade and Puma invest in their advertising campaigns? Well, you might not have that same scale of budget, but you can still follow their example by investing on a scale that is appropriate to your business.

Investment may mean time, or it may mean money. In most cases it means both – you just need to balance according to what works with your financial budget and what strategies are appropriate to the thing that you're promoting. Time includes researching your market and planning your marketing campaign, as well as any things you can do yourself, such as your social media campaigns. Money can go into direct marketing costs, including working with specialist consultants, as well as hard costs for paid advertising or printing.

Lather, rinse, and repeat...

Once you've successfully changed people's perception, what next? Then you just keep doing it. Keeping yourself and your products in the public awareness, and managing how you are perceived by the market, is an ongoing project. It never ends. If you are able to design some automated systems that track how your clients are finding you, that can help you understand which strategies work and which not to invest your money and time into – a real time- and money-saver.

As mentioned before, trends are ephemeral. They arise, sometimes seemingly from nowhere, and suddenly everyone is doing that or using it. And then, just as quick, that trend is out. No one would be caught dead wearing that, or using that, or listening to that! Gustavo was worried that Brook's designs were being copied. But Brook was lucky to have Sam reminding her that the trend was not going to last anyway, and that he was already working on their next great idea.

So you just have to be on it: following the steps listed above to get your product or concept out there, then massaging it so it becomes the next greatest thing and keeping it there as long as you can. Meanwhile, you must recognize that it's not going to last and already be working on your next idea or your next new thing.

Then you simply lather, rinse, and repeat.

Make it "talkaboutable"

Our final message about trendsetting is: Get people talking. The more naturally viral you can go, the better. Being "talkaboutable" is a result of both successful differentiation and good marketing. And this is where your influential people make a difference.

Did you know that one of the world's most famous composers, Johann Sebastian Bach, was not very famous in his own lifetime? Bach died in 1750. Up until that time, his music was known only to a few high-brow "connoisseurs." It wasn't until nearly a century later that another famous composer, Felix Mendelssohn, started what has come to be known as the "Bach Revival."

Keep in mind that this was happening in the days before the internet, before phones, even before being able to record music! The Bach Revival took place entirely as a result of word-of-mouth: people talking about Bach, creating a buzz. Within only a few years of Mendelssohn starting to talk about Bach, public opinion had turned around: Bach, formerly nearly unknown, had come to be regarded as one of the world's greatest composers – a reputation he still holds today, nearly two centuries later.

Staying ahead of the game

The big thing to remember about trends is that they *are* short-lived. They start abruptly and they don't stick around. So, it doesn't matter whether it was you or your major competitor who started whatever is trendy today; whatever it is, it's not going to last. So there's a few things you can do.

Look ahead

Keep working on what's next, looking ahead and observing. If your combination of hard work and a little bit of luck means that your last thing has caught on, well, that's no excuse for slacking off. Start thinking about your next thing. And if your thing didn't catch on, sorry, but you still have to be thinking about the next one.

What does the market want that current suppliers are not providing? Your market may not even realize that they want it yet. But if you can recognize what they are lacking and provide the solution, they will latch onto it.

For example, there is a new type of restaurant that targets people who dine alone: business travellers as well as busy working singles who don't have time to cook every night. These solo diners know they are the exception to the restaurant scene, which is mainly social, but they quietly fit themselves in. They head out to the milieu of noisy tables – families, partiers, birthday groups – avoiding eye contact and perhaps feeling a bit awkward that they are taking up a whole table themselves, as they try to get some work done or read a book.

But some brilliant forward-thinking person recognized these people's needs: a quiet restaurant where every table is spacious enough for files, or a book, or a laptop. A place where solo diners are the norm. It's a need that people didn't even know that they had, but once the product was offered to them, they realized that it was just what they had been missing.

Be daring

Sure, there is an element of luck in having a product or an idea getting picked up and becoming a trend. But what we want to emphasize is that it is not only luck. (If it was then why do the same people "get lucky" and be seen as the trendsetter or innovator or visionary over and over again? Think: Steve Jobs, Elon Musk, Mark Burnett, and more).

There are numerous things that you can do to increase the chances of your product being picked up and becoming a trend. Don't be discouraged by failure: you will probably have numerous misfires along the way. (Remember, the most successful people have failed many more times than the rest of the crowd – only because they have tried more.)

Also, being a trendsetter doesn't mean it has to be on a global scale! You might be a trendsetter in a small niche and only a small market knows about it. That market could be geographically small, like in your home town, or it could be conceptually small, like specialist ultra-lightweight racing bike accessories. Your product doesn't have to be global news to create a trend.

Look ahead, take chances, and be daring.

BONUS! Perception in Your Personal Life

B rook was exhausted. And starving. Sure, business was going well, but she hadn't even been able to stop for a lunch break. She slammed the door and kicked off her boots.

"Hi honey," Roger called. "I'm in the kitchen!"

Brook didn't answer. She threw her bag down on top of her boots and ambled into the kitchen.

"Hey honey," Roger leaned to kiss her on the cheek and then drew back. "Everything okay?"

"What's for dinner?"

"I was thinking we should maybe go out for Chinese," Roger replied. "What do you think?"

"Roger! It's your turn to cook!" She opened the fridge door and grabbed an open bottle of white from the door. "I do nearly all of the cooking. You've got two measly days a week!"

"But Brook, you love Chinese. I thought it would be fun."

She grabbed a glass from the shelf, and then turned and glared at him.

Roger took the glass from Brook's hand, reached for another and poured them each one. "We can still have a glass of wine first. I'm not in a rush."

Brook took her glass and sipped. "Whatever. Sure."

Roger's gaze had hardened. "Brook, you can't just come in here..."

"Roger, I've had a really tough day. I don't need it from you too. I'll be in my office. Call me when you want to go."

She stomped back to the front door. The files had spilled out from her bag and were spread across the mat. She set her wine down on the floor and reached for them. But somehow she knocked the glass. "Godammit!"

"Happy anniversary," said Max, and he placed a narrow rectangular box on the table.

Kylie looked puzzled. Then her face burst into a huge smile. "Our old anniversary!"

"Well, the new one is still too far away. I think the old one counts more anyway." He placed two glasses on the table. "Champagne?"

Kylie unwrapped the box and then Max placed the bracelet around her wrist. "Max, it's beautiful. But I feel guilty. I wasn't thinking of today. I don't have anything for you."

He passed her a glass. "Cheers," he said. "I know. It's a bit weird to surprise you with our old anniversary. But I also wanted to thank you ... because you have already given me so much."

"Well, we're partners now. Again. We both give," she said.

"In the relationship, yes," he replied. "But I mean also for my career. Your support, your expertise in marketing. The time you've put in to help me."

She smiled and sipped her champagne. "Yum, it's good." She swirled the glass and watched the bubbles dance upward before taking another sip.

"I mean it, Kylie," Max continued. "It was like I didn't have any direction. I didn't have any confidence any more. I felt like a loser ... didn't even want to try anything."

"Max," she said, and she put her hand on his. The bracelet on her wrist sparkled.

"But I just feel different now. I'm okay about taking chances. I know that what Eric and I are doing now is a risk; we might not succeed. But now I'm okay with that."

"You just need to trust yourself," Kylie said.

"I think that's the difference. You helped me start to do that. I feel good about who I am now. Even if this thing with Eric doesn't work out, there are other things I can try. I have so many ideas."

Kylie looked into his eyes and raised her glass. "Cheers, baby."

Brook watched the wine dribble across her file folders and down to her boots. It slowly absorbed into the matt. Bloody Roger. Why was she even so mad at him?

She picked up her glass and the soggy folders and went back to the kitchen. Roger handed her the paper towels.

"I'm sorry," she said. She wiped the folders and set them on the counter. Then she embraced him. She felt his body soften to hers and the bristles of his chin on the side of her neck. "I'm just really stressed. There's so much going on."

"Sweetheart," he whispered. He held her even tighter then stroked her hair. "Your company is growing really fast. But that's because you're so amazing."

Brook sunk her head into his shoulder. "I didn't even have lunch today."

"Well, no wonder you're such a grump," Roger said, but he laughed.

Brook laughed back. "Roger! You're supposed to be nice to me."

"Well, I did invite you out for dinner. But you got mad at me!" He stepped back and took the empty glass from her hand. "Can I pour you a new glass of wine? And then can we go eat some stir fry?"

"Can we do sushi instead?" asked Brook.

Roger smiled. "You're on!"

Danielle no longer felt nervous when she was called into the offices of the Misters Frank and Jones. In fact, her last few meetings with them had actually gone great.

"Thank you for coming in, ah, Danielle," started Mr. Jones. "Coffee?"

Danielle nodded, and Mr. Jones called for his assistant.

"Danielle," Mr Frank said. "Harold and I have been talking. We're very pleased with your work these past few months. You've been with us for a long time. We're not sure whether we've simply overlooked you or whether you have..."

"We like your ideas," interrupted Mr. Jones. "We like how you communicate with your peers. You're seen as a mentor, a resource."

Mr. Frank added, "You bring value to our team."

The assistant came in with a tray of coffee. Mr. Frank passed a cup to Danielle as he continued, "And we do like your ideas. Especially what you mentioned earlier – launching another branch focusing on small businesses."

"Yes, the entrepreneurs, the consultants," said Mr. Jones, reaching across the table for a cup. "I enjoyed your talk last week at the Chamber, by the way."

"Thank you," said Danielle.

"We would like to take you up on that idea," said Mr. Frank. "It would have to be a formal separate arm of the business. We don't want to dilute our message as we are doing really well with the large organizations."

"A new, ah, 'wing,' let's say," added Mr. Jones.

"What would that mean?" asked Danielle. "I mean, for me?"

"We would like you to be the leader. This would mean some sort of promotion for you, of course. But we still need to work out the details," said Mr. Jones. "We would like you to write a proposal for us, outlining how you would see this working. We could assign one of the boys to work with you."

Mr. Jones glanced at Mr. Frank. "Tony, if you're happy to have him?" Mr. Frank nodded.

Danielle gulped. This was a lot of responsibility. Being in charge of a whole new wing of the business? It was scary. But, she reminded herself, this is what she had been working toward.

Danielle smiled. "Tony's great. I'd be happy to work with him. I'll have a proposal for you next week."

Although much of this book is focused on the business world, nearly all of the information and advice in here is 100% applicable to you, personally, as well. Have you ever felt that people don't see you for who you really are? Do you sometimes feel that life just sucks, and that this is not how you want things to be? Do you find yourself being passed over for career opportunities, which end up going to people who you *know* are not as competent as you are? All of these personal problems can be improved via influencing perception.

Internal perception

We touched briefly upon the differences between the two types of perception – "internal perception" and "external perception" – in *Chapter 4* in the section about how you perceive and value yourself and how this can dictate your pricing structure. In this chapter, we're examining how the concepts behind perception influence your personal life, in addition to your business success.

External perception has been the focus of most of this book: how *others* perceive you and what you can do to change or influence that. Internal perception is how *you* view yourself: what you think of yourself and understand about yourself.

If your perception of yourself is that you are not worthy of success, well, you are probably not very likely to find yourself driving down that happy road any time soon. This is an issue that Max has been dealing with – and now overcoming. Whereas if your perception of yourself is "I can do this" or "I deserve this," you are far more likely to achieve that success (not to mention portray that perception to others, which will attract even *more* of what you want).

Our internal perception may or may not be the reality. It's easy to think you are not good at something and become anxious – even if you are one of the world's best! Some of the greatest artists have suffered from performance anxiety and stage fright, including actor Laurence Olivier and singer Barbra Streisand. But this also works the other way around. You've probably met people who think they are much better than they really are; those people who think they are amazing drivers or great lovers (when, really they're not).

Our internal perception begins developing in childhood. We are all unique individuals, each of us with our own history (and hang-ups), and our own way of responding to life-altering circumstances.

Those childhood personality-forming moments affect different people in different ways. For one person, being told by a school teacher that they will never amount to anything could massively damage that person's confidence, so that they never have the courage or the confidence to get out there and try to follow their dreams.

But another person might respond in the opposite way. They might just decide that the teacher doesn't know anything and dismiss the comment. That comment might even piss them off to the point that it inspires them to prove that teacher wrong! They are moved to get out there and show that teacher (and the world) how good they are, developing the skills, and therefore the confidence, to really go after their dreams. One person may be crushed by that negative comment, while another might go on to rise above all of their classmates because of it.

It may be hard to change ingrained patterns of looking at (or judging) ourselves. But changing our internal perception is possible.

Awareness is the first step. Conscious action comes next.

Reframing situations

We always have a choice as to how we perceive a situation. But for some reason, it's easy for us to fall to the side of negativity. You can't always change your circumstances, but you can always change your perception of those circumstances.

Let us tell you about one of our good friends, Hannah.

Hannah had a decent job with a decent salary. She was living in a great little pad and had some fabulous friends.

Nevertheless, Hannah always found herself complaining and whining about everything and anything. Her perception of her life was that it sucked, even though her friends' perception of Hannah's life was that she had it all!

Then Hannah met a guy who took her on a trip through South America. One day, as she was sitting in a little village in the middle of nowhere in Bolivia, she asked herself why everyone seemed so happy there. These people had almost nothing! They didn't even know where their food would come from, one day to the next. Yet they seemed to have this infectious contentment about life.

That experience really got Hannah thinking. She came to realize that it really does come down to perception. If you think you are missing out or lacking, that's how your life will be, no matter how much money or success you have.

Reframing your perception also works on a day-to-day level. For example, let's say you had a really bad day at work and are in a super-grumpy mood. It's pretty easy to carry that negative attitude into the home with you – and what happens? When Brook came in all grumpy from a stressful day at work, she got in a fight with her husband. Did that make her day any better? No!

But Brook realized what she'd done. By reframing the situation, and **choosing** not to make a bad thing worse, she apologized to Roger and explained to him what was going on for her and how she felt. By reframing things, and not carrying negativity around, Brook contributed to making a bad situation better, and put an end to their fight.

You've probably heard of the technique of visualization. Well here's an exercise. Try this someday if you are feeling a bit down. Imagine yourself as the happiest, most energized person in the world. Really see it in your mind, and **feel** it. Then act like you are happy and energized, even for just two minutes, and you **will** feel better. It takes a bit of practice, and it may not happen right away, but you **can** influence your own perception of how you feel and gradually turn it into your reality.

Here's another thing to try. (It may sound silly, but don't worry - no one will see!) If you're driving home, about to bring your bad day into the family home (like Brook did), turn up your music and have a car dance party all by yourself. Or make yourself squawk like a chicken three times as loud as you can ... really, really loud, so you make yourself laugh a little. You can change things very quickly and walk in your door in a totally different frame of mind.

Becoming the desired you

Nobody is perfect! Absolutely everyone has some scope to improve on who they are (most of us a lot!).

We all have some insecurities. As we discussed above, much of that comes from childhood. But it doesn't mean we can't change. We're afraid of failure, so we don't want to try. We are afraid of criticism, so we don't put ourselves out there. We are afraid that people will laugh at us, or that we will fall – all of these things hold us back.

If you perceive yourself as a failure, or that you are worthless, you are not likely to seek out opportunities. It becomes a kind of self-fulfilling prophecy. The people who see themselves as successful are out there trying – and actually failing a lot – but they keep trying because they believe that they are worth it, they deserve it, and some day it will work out. Some even begin to enjoy the failure ... weird, right? If you know it's taking you closer to a win then it's all progress and part of the fun.

Who ends up achieving success? Those who are trying, of course: the ones who perceive themselves as successful, despite their numerous failures!

Of course, success comes down to each individual's perception of what success actually means. We work with many businesses of all shapes and sizes, and just because someone has a very large turnover definitely doesn't mean they are happy. Some smaller business owners might do smaller turnovers but spend four months per year travelling with their family and love their business.

Take a look at your own self-perception and see if there are any differences between the person you **perceive** yourself to be and the person you **want** to be. If your perception is holding you back, changing that self-perception is the first step to becoming the person you want to be – and deserve to be.

Attracting your kind of people

The examples above relate to internal perception: how you see yourself. But you don't walk this earth in isolation. Other people are important to you, too, both in your personal life and in your professional life.

You can use most of the techniques of external perception that we have presented throughout this book to influence what **others** think of you: to attract the kind of people that you want to be around you and to form the types of relationships you desire. These techniques work just as well in the personal world as they do in the business world.

Remember, of course, not to try to create any sort of perception that is false – that's not the point! Always remain genuine and true to yourself when creating your external perception. Putting out a fake image may achieve you temporary success, but it will never last in the long term. Amplify what you already are and what the world needs to know!

What kind of people do you want in your life? You may want to hang out with the artists, or with the triathletes, or with other parents of young children. Look at Max. There *are* people who want to be around him, but they are not the types of people he *wants* to be around. He was attracting the wrong crowd. But now he is changing how people perceive him and, therefore, the kinds of people he attracts, both as fans and in his personal life. Attracting the right people also includes saying no to people you don't want in your life.

To do this, you first need to define the type of people you want to hang with, and then find where they are. Once you have located them, you need to influence their perception of you, so they see you as one of their "tribe" and want to include you in what they are doing.

For example, let's say you've been at your fairly new job in a corporate office for a few months now. A group of employees has formed an informal hiking group and they head out on the trails on the weekends. Every Monday, they come in talking about that weekend's adventure. You dearly want to go, but you don't feel comfortable asking them directly. Although you've dropped some serious hints, you've still never been invited.

Think about it from their side, though. What is their perception of you? It may never have occurred to them that you are a hiker. If they have only ever seen you in your tidy office wear, and you only talk about work, they might have the perception that you are not very outdoorsy. Maybe even "high-maintenance" on the trails.

Perhaps you need to change their perception of you: putting some wilderness photos up in your office, or simply telling them about various hikes you've done. If you can change that perception they have of you, you are more likely to score an invite.

Attracting more opportunities

How you are perceived works as much for realizing success in your career as it does in your personal life. It doesn't matter if you are the most qualified and competent person in the office: if your bosses don't see you that way, you are not going to be the one getting the promotion. It doesn't matter if you have done all of your market research and have a great business plan: if you come across looking unprofessional or as if you don't have a handle on your finances, your banker is not going to feel comfortable granting you a loan.

Danielle has made some positive steps in improving how she is perceived in the office. By deciding to make the effort to mentor Tony and Hatsuo, she is not only improving personal skills she was lacking in (confidence, communication), she is also creating a very favorable perception to her bosses – that she is generous, knowledgeable, and a team player. She is creating the perception that she has value and is someone they want to keep around. And look how that changed perception is sending her up the career ladder!

You not only have to *be* good to get ahead in your career, you also have to **create the perception that you are good.** One goes with the other. If you only have one or the other, it's not likely that you will advance your career. The people who make decisions about your opportunities and your future need to **know** what your attributes are, and what your value to them is.

Now, Make it Happen!

Brook and Roger weaved their way across the field. It was full of people – some sitting on the grass near the front, some on lawn chairs they had brought, and others seated around plastic tables near the back. Max and Eric were on stage and a group were dancing at the front of the field, next to them.

"Oh, they've already started," said Brook. She spied Danielle, Cedric, and Kylie at one of the tables. "Over there," she pointed.

Danielle greeted them with a smile. "Hey Roger, you finally made it out with us."

Roger joked back, "Yup, they're actually letting me stay home for a few weeks."

Brook turned to Cedric as they took their seats. "Are we late? I didn't think they'd be playing already."

"Max and Eric are just opening," answered Cedric. "Max has a new group he's managing. He wanted them to headline."

"*Three* new groups," added Kylie. "Managing and producing is really taking off for him."

"Max has become a great support for *Habitanto*," said Cedric, looking around. "We sold nearly two thousand tickets for this. Not to mention, he's doing the soundtrack for the next film."

"What he and Eric are doing is really taking off," said Kylie. "Their indie-electronica thing. People love it. And all these musicians are asking him to work with them."

"That's fantastic," said Roger. He turned to Brook. "Brook has some news too."

Brook was glowing. "I'm going to Japan next month!"

"To work with that architect?" asked Danielle.

"Yes!" exclaimed Brook. "Working on some preliminary designs for a building in London! And also doing some purchasing."

"Brooklyn Winston is going global!" grinned Roger. "She's thinking about Bolivia for next year too."

Cedric raised his beer glass. "Looks like we've got good news all around. Because Danielle didn't just get promoted to any old new job. Frank & Jones actually *created* the new job just for her. In fact, they created a whole new arm of the company!"

"You got it, Dani!" Brook exclaimed. "Well deserved! About time they recognized what you do."

Max finished his set and was packing up. He spoke quickly to the singer from the next band then caught Kylie's eye from the stage.

"Max will be here in a minute," Kylie said. "Let's save our cheers until he gets here."

"Sure," said Danielle. She turned to Brook. "I know. It's like they finally see me differently. See me for who I am. And value me more."

"That's how I feel too," answered Brook. "We always had these great products. But it was also always a struggle. Then all of a sudden everyone realized what we're about. And suddenly it's easy."

Brook glanced at Roger. "Except I can hardly keep up with it all." He smiled back at her.

"Well, that's kind of like Max too," Kylie said, as Max slid into the seat beside her and pecked her on the cheek. "People saw him one way, but that wasn't how he really was. And now they see him for what he is, and he's way happier. Right, baby?"

Max smiled and Cedric picked up his glass again. Brook, Roger, Danielle, Max, and Kylie raised theirs as well. "Cheers, my friends," Cedric toasted. "To your many successes."

So get out there and change perception!

Well, you've made it to the end of this book. Thanks for sticking with us! Here are some final words on how to use all of the information we have presented here, no matter what your situation is.

Keeping it reasonable

First of all, be reasonable with your expectations. Trying to change your whole perception may not be achievable – at least not right away. Identify what circumstances you can influence and be realistic about identifying any that perhaps you have little or no possibility of changing. Place all of your focus and efforts on the ones that you can influence, and detach yourself from those you can't.

Making time for it all

You most likely don't have infinite time, energy, or resources. (Wouldn't it be nice if you did?) So focus your efforts on the strategies that will yield the highest results for effort expended.

To do this, make a list of everything you are doing right now to influence your perception. This could include your marketing campaign, such as paid advertisements, your website or your social media presence, as well as your overall "look" or brand personality, like the design of your storefront or how your employees are instructed to communicate with clients.

Trying to change everything at once leads to a diluted effort that may not yield any results. So pick 10% of what's on your list and focus your efforts only on those things until they are at the level that you want. For example, right now you might decide only to work on updating your LinkedIn profile and redesigning your product packaging.

Once you have completed those tasks, look at the next 10%. Keep working this way until you have completed everything on your list. But don't think you're done there! Review and revise that to-do list. Perhaps there are new things that need attention, or maybe that LinkedIn profile is already due for another update. Remember, you must monitor continuously then drop what is not working and amplify what is.

Tracking what works

Have you heard of the 80/20 rule? It's that typically 20% of your efforts will yield 80% of your results. This applies to creating perception too.

However, we usually don't know in advance which of the things on our list will fall into that 20%. So try to track your results so that you will learn with time where to focus your efforts for best advantage. You can do this by website tracking (for example, finding out where your visitors have come from, what search words they used, or which pages work best for converting views to sales) as well as by feedback forms asking clients where they heard about you.

Becoming irresistible

Remember, your goal is irresistibility. You want people to want you, want your products, and want your services. Passionately, uncontrollably.

Being "the real deal" is of ultimate importance. Of course, you must produce or provide a quality product or service! Never stop being genuine or real.

However, quality alone is not enough to guarantee that your business will flourish – or even survive. Remember, Dolly Parton lost her own contest because other people managed their perception better. There's no point in working so hard to be the real deal, yet losing the game in spite of that.

Irresistibility is all about perception. Perception is what will make people come to you or desire you. Yes, you must do whatever you do well. **But you must also let the world know that.** The strategies we've outlined in this book will set you on that path.

That's it. We're pretty much there. Next is for you to get out there and start applying the information in this book to succeed. Achieve success in your career, sell your product or service, start or run or expand your business, and live the life you want to live.

So get out there and do it!

And keep in touch!

We trust you've found the information in this book useful. Please stay in touch and let us know what worked for you, and what ideas or input you have for us. You'll find additional materials on this book's web page—www.basicbananas.com/perception—and we'd love to hear your comments or help you if you have any questions.

We've already mentioned one of our businesses – *Basic Bananas* – a marketing training organization. We work with all types of companies, but we place a special emphasis on small business owners. If you would like to learn more about our clever approaches to marketing, or our worldwide marketing mentoring programs, visit our website www.basicbananas.com.

We also have a sister company called *The Business Hood*, which focuses on developing your own brand strategy to make sure you get noticed. If you are interested in branding, a design overhaul, or a new website or logo, please check out www.thebusinesshood.com.

If you need engaging speakers on subjects related to marketing and entrepreneurship, we can cater our popular presentations specifically to your crowd, from small business events to corporate functions to large conferences. Take a look at the keynote presentations we offer at www.franziskaandchristo.com or contact us directly at speaking@basicbananas.com.

And of course, make sure you stay in touch with us via your preferred social media channels. You'll find us at:

- Facebook www.facebook.com/basicbananas
- Twitter: @basicbananas @franziskaiseli @christohall
- Instagram @basicbananas @franziskaiseli @christohall
- LinkedIn: Basic Bananas
- YouTube: BasicBananasDotCom (we have lots of free instructional videos here)

We look forward to hearing from you!

MORE PRODUCTS AND PROGRAMS BY THE AUTHORS

Bananas About Marketing
– How to attract a whole bunch of happy clients

Bananas About Marketing is a much-needed breath of fresh air in the marketing and small business world. Growing a business can be challenging at the best of times, but Franziska Iseli and Christo Hall present a new approach that is fresh, fun, and cheeky, and definitely takes out the "pain factor"! This book is like no other. Using practical examples, simple strategies, and an entertaining storyline, it shows you how to attract the right clients and fast track your business to success so you can live the lifestyle of your dreams. Let's face it, isn't that why you're in business in the first place?

Available at www.amazon.com or www.basicbananas.com/bananasaboutmarketing

Blast-Off Marketing Workshop

In this short, jam-packed workshop the Basic Bananas team pull back the curtains on the most effective ways to attract clients. The fastest way to grow your business is to use clever marketing! The good news is that it's not really rocket science, but there are a few key elements you must know to avoid a scattered approach to marketing. *Marketing Blast-Off* is an intensive half-day workshop where you will discover the steps to make your business stand out from the crowd, attract new clients, and add more money to the bottom line. These workshops are available globally. Please visit *www.basicbananas.com/blast-off* to find the nearest location!

The Online Eco System – Online Marketing Course

This program demystifies online marketing for business owners. Discover the online eco-system to create online marketing campaigns for your business. This is a free step-by-step course, which will guide you to take your online marketing to a whole new level. Download this program here: *www.basicbananas.com/ecosystem*

Subscribe to Basic Bananas Radio

Every week, the founders of Basic Bananas release a new radio episode you can access via iTunes. The show delivers nothing but extremely valuable tips and tricks specifically for small business owners. Open your podcast App, search for Basic Bananas and hit subscribe.

The Clever Bunch Program

The Clever Bunch is a step-by-step twelve months program with monthly live workshops to create a marketing machine that brings in a constant flow of clients.

www.basicbananas.com/cleverbunch

The Marketing Smarts

The Marketing Smarts is an online training and mentoring program to grow your business, using a combination of online and offline marketing strategies.

www.themarketingsmarts.com

ABOUT THE AUTHORS

Franziska Iseli is a maverick entrepreneur, leading marketing and brand strategist, speaker, author and the co-founder of BasicBananas.com, OceanLovers.global, YoursSocially.com, TheBusinessHood.com and Impacteurs.com.

In 2013 Franziska was awarded the Young Entrepreneur of the Year Award recognizing her innovation, creativity, and philanthropic involvement.

A true visionary, no challenge seems to be too big for Franziska. She is known for her rebellious nature and challenging the norm. She has this rare combination of being both creative and strategic, which makes her a powerful thought leader in the business world.

The key to Franziska's success is her down-to-earth attitude, infectious energy, integrity, and fearlessness to take the lead. As a Swiss-born Aussie with a sharp-witted humor, and the ability to speak five languages, she has also been known to make up a few words.

Franziska is a big believer in social business and is always on the lookout for social projects; the latest ones include the adoption of a Mongolian wild horse and a whale.

To find out more visit www.franziskaiseli.com or connect with her via different social media channels @franziskaiseli.

Christo Hall is a clever entrepreneur, online marketing strategist, speaker, author, and the co-founder of BasicBananas.com and TheBusinessHood.com.

When it comes to nifty marketing tips and tricks to attract new business, Christo is the man. He has helped thousands of business owners to create powerful strategies, add millions in additional income, and build scalable marketing systems.

Christo has always been very entrepreneurial (He claims to never have had a 'real' job.), learning how to make money and appealing to clients at a young age. After being a full-time professional surfer for eight years, he became a full-time entrepreneur (working part time) and hasn't looked back since.

Christo is known for his out-of-the-box thinking and leadership, and doesn't play by the rules of convention.

To find out more visit www.christohall.com or connect with him via different social media channels @christohall.

Franziska and Christo are world-renowned speakers and regularly present at some of the largest conferences around the globe including TEDx. Their advice is regularly sought by the media and they have been featured across different publications including the Sydney Morning Herald, The Huffington Post, Channel 9, BRW, and 2UE.

To book **Franziska** and **Christo** for
your next event, please visit
www.franziskaandchristo.com